THE CORBETT PAPERS

The Corbett Papers

Biographical, Legal, &
Contextual Material on
the Life & Career of Jim Corbett of Kumaon

compiled and edited by

AKSHAY SHAH

& STEPHEN ALTER

The Corbett Papers, first published in hardback 2022
by Black Kite (an imprint of Permanent Black)
This paperback edition published in 2024 by Black Kite

in association with

Hachette India
(an Hachette UK company)

All editorial management by Black Kite

ISBN: 978-93-5731-693-4

10 9 8 7 6 5 4 3 2

Black Kite/Permanent Black, D28 Oxford Apartments,
11 IP Extension, Delhi 110092

Hachette Book Publishing India Pvt. Ltd
4th & 5th Floors, Corporate Centre
Plot No. 94, Sector 44, Gurugram – 122003, India

Printed and bound in India by
Manipal Technologies Limited

for

Kala Mama who mentored me
my parents who nurtured me
and my beloved wife Renu for always being there
A.S.

Contents

Introduction

Remembering Corbett's Biographer, D.C. Kala

AKSHAY SHAH

It was late spring in April 1981 when my maternal uncle took me, along with my brothers and cousins, to Naukuchiatal during our Easter break. We were going to spend our holidays at the home of his friend, Mr D.C. Kala. Mr Kala, after retiring from the *Hindustan Times* in New Delhi, had rented the ground floor of a bungalow surrounded by forest and overlooking the pristine Naukuchiatal lake.

That was the first time I met Mr Kala and, being my uncle's friend, he was always Kala Mama to me thereafter. I instantly took a liking to this old man. He had a truculent exterior and was a little detached with all the other children. I was just eleven then, and he was in his early sixties. My first memories of him are of a wise old man who always wore a *lungi* at home, rolling his cigarettes from Capstan paper and a Wills tobacco pouch. His house was frugally furnished and sparsely decorated but I remember a sketch of Mahakaal adorning one wall, a lot of books on a shelf, and an almirah.

After living a couple of years at Naukuchiatal, Kala Mama moved into a cottage next to ours at Eton House in Nainital. There I grew closer to him. He took me under his tutelage and opened the world of natural history to me. Feeling special, an unbridled joy washed over me each time he summoned me to accompany him on long walks in the forest. We spent hours together making cider from Rimer apples. My first tot of rum with him was when I cleared my Class 10 board exam and he let me spend many quiet hours in his sitting room poring over his books. Then there were the many delightful evenings together when he enraptured me with personal anecdotes, baffled me with the intricacies of dry fly fishing or the nuances of mysticism, and enthused me with thoughts on wildlife and wild flowers while casually cooking finger-licking pork chops that we devoured together.

Kala Mama was all this and much more to me. He was a treasure trove of knowledge. As a sprightly 65-year-old, he took me on my first long trek to the Pindari Glacier and introduced me to the outdoors – to which I have ever since been hooked.

Kala Mama was born in Nainital on 2 July 1921 as Durga Charan Kala. He described himself as a naturalist, a lover of the wilderness and of wide open spaces. His father, Sri Govind Ram Kala, was a civil servant based in Kumaon, where Kala Mama had spent his early years – in spacious bungalows, on a tea garden, and even in an old fort. At the age of twelve he built himself a tree house. After finishing his Master's in geography from Aligarh Muslim University, he took up journalism and in 1945 started as an apprentice with the *Leader* (Allahabad), ending his career with the *Hindustan Times* (New Delhi).

After Nainital he, ever restless, moved off to Panyali, a village on the outskirts of Ranikhet. Here he lived for a short time before renting "Trevone", a cottage in the Ranikhet cantonment. Finally, he settled down in a little cottage within a large estate called "Himalayana" owned by the publisher Ravi Dayal. Here he was surrounded by stately deodars, wild flowers and birds, and was our neighbour again – our house was a short ten-minute walk from his.

My mentoring continued. I would spend hours sitting with him, nursing pegs of Old Monk while he reminisced and regaled me with old episodes about himself, his youth, his father or mother, or inspired me with his vast knowledge on various subjects. Evenings would fade away into night, the birdcalls would stop, the quiet forest would embark upon its night sounds, and I would inevitably be late reaching home.

Kala Mama was a disciple of Gopal-da and Ashish-da of Mirtola Ashram in Uttar Vrindavan – just short of Jageshwar in the Almora district of Uttarakhand – and frequented the Ashram whenever he could get away from his job in Delhi. On one such visit in the early 1970s, he had been constantly talking about Jim Corbett with his guru, Ashish-da – the famous Scottish sage Sri Madhava Ashish who had settled in the Himalaya. Later, when bidding him farewell to go back to Delhi, Ashish-da remarked, "All the best with your Corbett book." This came as a kind of epiphany: Kala Mama was, in a way, stuck with writing the first biography of Jim Corbett as it was his guru's *aadesh*. The following years were spent researching, both in India and England, and finally the first definitive biography of Jim Corbett was published in 1979 by Ankur Publishing House. Twenty years later, in 1999, his landlord in Ranikhet, Ravi Dayal, republished the book under his own imprint, "Ravi Dayal Publisher". It was an appropriate second home for Kala Mama's book: apart from the fact that his publisher was his landlord, Ravi Dayal's logo was an owl, and Dayal himself was a Kumaoni schooled in Himalayan folklore who had once come face to face with Jim Corbett in Nainital.

Kala Mama travelled extensively in the Himalaya, which he loved, including in the Kullu valley, up the Bhagirathi to its source, and Roopkund. In 1954 he was one of the first visitors permitted into the Corbett National Park, then known as Hailey National Park. The reputed naturalist E.P. Gee and Kala Mama were both instrumental in getting the park reopened to the public. Ever the naturalist, he travelled to Bharatpur, Periyar, Madumalai, Bandipur, Kaziranga, and the faraway Kerala Highlands.

He was not a great fan of mechanisation and throughout his life owned only two machines – a cycle and a typewriter. His typewriter was an oddity. It was either antique enough or handicapped enough to be equipped with only capital letters, and on this Kala Mama typed out the entire manuscripts of both his books, *Jim Corbett of Kumaon* and *Hulson Sahib of Garhwal* (the second a biography of the British logging entrepreneur Frederick Wilson who went native in Harsil and ruled the region as a local raja). As a seasoned newspaperman, Kala Mama went meticulously over his "Thus Capital", inserting editorial marks in ink before sending it off to the publisher.

Though he came across as a person of rough countenance and somewhat forbidding exterior, Kala Mama had a very pleasing demeanour and his house was always a welcome refuge for all. Visitors were unfailingly offered a drink of his favourite Old Monk rum – in fact we joked that he was the best advertisement for the brand – an old monk drinking an Old Monk! A voracious reader, he loved his solitude and would not hesitate to ask visitors to "vanish" if they overstayed. Lovingly called Mahatma by his dear friends, he was stubbornly independent and refused all help, even over his last days. He passed away on 14 May 2007 and was cremated in Ranikhet's verdant cemetery, through which a mountain spring flows. While he lived, he was truly the enigmatic, widely venerated, and grand old man of Ranikhet.

The little cottage where he spent his last years was very stark, its furniture sparse, a far cry from his former Delhi lifestyle. A small porch led to a room which opened into a tiny kitchenette. The only cooking implements he had were an LPG stove and a *silbatta* (grinding stone), besides the regular pots and utensils. As one entered the main room, a single cot stood on one side with a small peg table next to it flaunting an overused table lamp. The windows were draped in luxurious off-white designer curtains, the sole remnants of his affluent past. An old steel trunk adorned with a tablecloth served as the drawing room table, with two chairs facing the cot making up the seating space. Besides a terracotta ashtray there would always be his tobacco pouch and the cigarette paper, and close at hand a bottle of water. On the trunk there lay his comfort zone – a pile of newspapers and the book he was reading or re-reading or researching.

Two bookshelves in the drawing room were filled with literary treasures. A wooden almirah contained his clothes and the other side of the room was lined with some trunks and a large leather suitcase. These held the manuscripts, articles, newspaper cuttings, research work, Corbett's and Frederick Wilson's papers, and an assortment of pipes which he had collected over the years. Next to them stood a simple wooden table graced only by a single museum piece – his infamous typewriter – and a rickety wooden chair. He was a minimalist and lived the life of the true hermit that he was.

Being his literary heir, I inherited all his research papers, notes, and manuscripts, some of which are reproduced here.

MUSSOORIE, FEBRUARY 2022

I

A Life Retold

“The Story” by D.C. Kala

Several authors have attempted to tell the story of Jim Corbett's life. The first was Marjorie Clough, an American Red Cross Volunteer who, at some point during World War II, was commissioned by the New York office of Oxford University Press (OUP) to meet Corbett in Agra and later at Kaladhungi, where she interviewed him and his sister Maggie. Her brief biographical sketch was incorporated into OUP's publicity materials, promoting Corbett's books in the United States. Geoffrey Cumberlege, Corbett's editor at OUP (London), used some of Clough's research and his own interviews with Jim and Maggie, as well as their letters, to compile a short life history that was never published, though much of this material found its way into Cumberlege's introduction to the World's Classics edition of *Man-Eaters of Kumaon* (1960). In addition to these are Maggie's recorded reminiscences, which were dictated in Kenya to her friend Ruby Beyts and are reproduced in this volume.

The first book-length biography was written by Durga Charan Kala and published in 1979 by Ankur Publishing House. This was followed, several years later, by Martin Booth's *Carpet Sahib*, published by Constable & Co. in London in 1986, and then brought out in India by OUP in 1990. When D.C. Kala moved from Delhi to Ranikhet, he happened to rent a cottage from a publisher, Ravi Dayal, who offered to edit and reissue the book, which came out in 1999 with the title *Jim Corbett of Kumaon*. It was later jointly republished by Penguin Books India and Ravi Dayal in 2009.

The first chapter of *Jim Corbett of Kumaon*, titled "The Story", is reproduced here both as an introduction to Corbett's life and his success as a writer, as well as a sample of D.C. Kala's approach and style. Kala spent a great deal of time collecting information for his biography. He met and corresponded with Corbett's primary editor in India, R.E. Hawkins, and procured a copy of Ruby Beyts' typescript, as well as Jim Corbett's Will. Being from the lower Himalaya himself and having grown up in Kumaon, where his father was a civil servant, Kala also had access to a variety of individuals who remembered Corbett or were in possession of various documents and memorabilia. Much of his book is based on these primary sources as well as letters, reviews, and newspaper clippings.

Because D.C. Kala worked for many years as a writer and editor at the *Hindustan Times*, he approached his subject with the perseverance of a journalist following multiple leads that were later braided together into a coherent story. Being an avid naturalist himself, he had first-hand knowledge of the many species of plants, trees, birds, and animals that Corbett describes in his books. Kala's writing style is unique and at times the book verges on a stream-of-consciousness narrative that his editor must have controlled and directed. Perhaps the most enjoyable part of the book is the way in which it plunders the mythology and lore of Corbett's life and combines these with Kala's own eccentric opinions and embellishments. Whether Corbett himself would have approved of such a biography is hard to say, but in many ways the two men were fellow raconteurs whose voices echo one another.

The Story

The First Chapter of D.C. Kala's *Jim Corbett of Kumaon**

The setting of this book is two continents – Asia, which raised Lieutenant-Colonel Edward James Corbett, IARO, VD, OBE, CIE,[1] Kaiser-i-Hind; and Africa, which gathered him to its arms in death. His triumphs were distributed between two countries, India and Kenya. Except for the last seven years of his life, he lived in India, a tiger among men, lover of the underdog, a hero in war and pestilence, a model zamindar and employer, an ascetic, naturalist, and, above all, a hunter of man-eating tigers and leopards for thirty-two active years in the three hill districts of Uttar Pradesh comprising Garhwal, Naini Tal and Almora. Others hunted, but he also wrote. Of his seven books *Man-Eaters of Kumaon*, a breathless whirl through tiger-land, got him millions of fans and a top niche as a narrator of true jungle stories. In the realm of high adventure, he is a man of the five continents where his fans are and will be.

*Our thanks to Ravi Dayal Publishers for permission to quote this extract.

[1] Indian Army Reserve of Officers (IARO); VD, a decoration for voluntary officers; Officer of the Order of the British Empire (OBE); Companion of the Indian Empire (CIE).

Except for a lone triumph, Africa was a continent of sorrow for him. He stayed there, dogged by ill-health, as a refugee after the exit of the British Raj from India, unsure of the changing times, the White sahib looking for another colony. True, his two closest relations were there and also his friends – we shall come to them later. The hero's exit from the Indian scene was silent. None of his tenants knew their landlord was going, nor did the hundreds of poor Whites and near-Whites who stayed behind in Kumaon. The secret was let out only to a few friends.

Corbett was admired in his hometown, Naini Tal, an unassuming man greeting high and low, exuding bonhomie. As a city father for no less than twenty-eight years, he is well remembered for keeping the forested area of the town intact from vandals. His tenants adored him. And all over the hill districts of Kumaon the legend of the hunter lives on in a dozen folk songs and a thousand tales of 'Carpet' Sahib. The Prime Minister-to-be of the province, G.B. Pant, was a crony of his with whom he spent hours (whenever Pant was in town and out of prison), swapping yarns of the Tarai, where both had worked and lived. He was the only Congressman Corbett liked. At least in one land deal he was Corbett's lawyer too.

Corbett's heart was always in Kumaon, in the village of Kaladhungi where he had his winter home, and in Naini Tal, high up fifteen miles away, where he lived in summer. 'I'd like to be reborn in Kumaon,' he would often say. Ensconced in the Baden-Powell cottage of the Outspan Hotel, Nyeri, off the Aberdare National Park in the Kenya Highlands, he sat worrying about his former tenants – he had freed them when he left – giving advice to a friend suffering from beri-beri, sending a fountain pen to a friend's son on his passing the Bachelor of Arts examination, wanting to take back the house (now the Corbett museum) he sold at Kaladhungi for the benefit of his tenants and dutifully sending till the end the land rent of Rs 910 a year on behalf of his tenants to the government.

From Kenya, he swapped notes with E.P. Gee, a brother naturalist (*Wild Life of India*), on the tigers of Hailey National Park, which Gee visited in 1954. And he compared notes on the Mau Mau and the Indian freedom movement. He was spared the indignity of seeing the exit of the Raj from Kenya though. Kenya became free in 1963 after sixty-eight years of White rule. Corbett died on 19 April 1955. But his sister, Margaret Winifred Corbett, who stuck to him till the end, saw the exodus.

India remembered Corbett by renaming its first national park after him in 1957. This was Hailey National Park, set up in 1935. In the first flush of freedom, while the tide of nationalism crested, it was found necessary to erase the memory of the builders of the Raj, and the Park was harmlessly renamed Ramganga National Park in 1955 after the river which formed its northern boundary. The government would have perhaps immortalised Corbett's friend, who became prime minister of U.P., but Pant stepped aside and helped in renaming it after Corbett.

I am sure Corbett would have been embarrassed to take over the Park, once named after Malcolm Hailey, Governor of the United Provinces in 1928–30 and 1931–34, a friend of his and a keen conservationist. Hailey outlived Corbett by at least fifteen years. Corbett was dead when the renaming came. And what could be a more fitting memorial than a tract of 324 square kilometres (now 528.4) in the Himalayan foothills for the tiger to survive in, I hope forever? Pant too got several memorials, including the renaming of the Ramsay Hospital at Naini Tal after him. This was the great Henry Ramsay who came to Kumaon in 1837 and ruled it for twenty-eight years as its sixth Commissioner. An early builder of the Raj, he was responsible for hundreds of projects and a thousand good deeds.

Corbett and his Premier friend, two of Naini Tal's best known sons, share 1,000 square yards of land on the Flats, as the upper end of the lake is known. Pant stands on a pedestal. His statue is black and larger than life. Corbett stands by the water unobtrusively and unknown in the form of a bandstand for which he donated Rs 7,300 in 1919 for the 'benefit of Naini Tal'. The hunter and angler is where the water is. The politician has his back on half the town and faces the other half where the road begins down-hill to the dusty plains. Few know the history of the bandstand, but Gurney House on Ayarpata Hill, which Corbett's sister Margaret Winifred (Maggie) inherited from her mother, is well known. He lived in this house before he left for Kenya. A third son of Naini Tal who left his mark but no monument was Gen. Orde Charles Wingate, the Chindit, who died in an air crash in Burma in 1944.

The 'Corbett museum' at his village of Choti Haldwani, near Kaladhungi, came later, a pitiable effort of the state Forest Department to perpetuate the hunter's memory by displaying some photographs and letters he wrote to Indian friends. This too was done in the Premier's days. The odds and ends displayed there are what the villagers have rifled from the untenanted house. The government acquired the house, restored it and set up a museum. Our man was generous with his minor trophies, and the Forest Department has not been able to collect the major ones, for these were auctioned by the executors of his will in Nairobi and are scattered all over the globe.

World recognition from brother naturalists came in 1968 with the naming of a subspecies of tiger after Corbett. This is *Panthera tigris corbetti*, found in Indo-China and extreme South China. It is slightly shorter than the Indian tiger and characterized by a 'darker ground coloration and more numerous, rather short stripes'. It was named after Corbett by Dr Vratislav Mazak to honour the 'excellent naturalist who devoted his life to the study and protection of Indian wildlife, particularly the tigers.'[2]

I spoke earlier of a personal triumph of Corbett's in Africa. That came in 1952, a few years before his death. He was privileged to escort Princess Elizabeth, who later ascended the British throne as Queen Elizabeth II, to Tree Tops Hotel in the Aberdare Mountains, near Nyeri, on a sightseeing safari a day before her father's death. Right from 1919, when he finished with the railways and practically retired to be a gentleman of leisure and businessman, ending up with a considerable fortune by the prevailing standards, he was in the foothill forests every winter with governors, collectors and at least one viceroy, hobnobbing with them, gun or fishing rod in hand.

Every collector of the district or forest officer who shot and fished became a friend. So did the maharajas, Jind for one. Young

[2] *Extrait de Mammalia*, Tome 32, No. 1.

White rookies posted to the district turned to him for their first lessons in tiger hunting. Because of his association with the top district officers he commanded considerable influence in the area. A Corbett complaint was always heard. To Kaladhungi he had a museum approach. He wanted it unspoiled, with himself as patriarch to whom all could turn for help.

Born on 25 July 1875, Corbett spent his childhood at Kaladhungi and Naini Tal. He was educated at Naini Tal. After school, he went straight to Bihar to work on the railways for twenty-three years. In 1914, when World War I broke out, he returned to Kumaon to raise a labour contingent for the British Army and served in France and Waziristan. After World War I, he settled down at Naini Tal, where he lived almost continuously till 1947, except for several trips to Tanganyika (modern Tanzania) and a stint during World War II training Allied troops in jungle war as Lieutenant-Colonel. As a city father of Naini Tal, he stepped into his father's shoes. The rest of the time he kept watch on all the bad tigers and leopards of the high hills and the adjoining plains.

These big, bad cats, maneaters to be precise, were Corbett's extra charge. When one was proclaimed a maneater by the district authorities, they turned to him for help to rid them of it. Sometimes the call came from stricken villagers themselves. Several requests even reached Mokameh Ghat, Bihar, where he worked during his railway days. He always agreed. Tracking and killing maneaters needs considerable skill and daring. The maneating leopard of Rudraprayag he killed was responsible for the death of 125 persons in a reign of terror of eight years in northern Garhwal. Another less-publicised leopard, the maneater of Panar, took 400 human lives.

When the call came, the 40-pound tent, the suitcase and the bedroll were hurriedly packed by sister Maggie, the porters were collected and the hunter set out in forced marches of twenty to forty miles a day – depending on the urgency – to the dak bungalow nearest to the last reported kill. Often, even after the last day's long march, he denied himself rest, left kit and porters at the dak bungalow and made a beeline to the kill or checked the lay of the land. If the kill was fresh enough, he would select a tree overlooking it, seek out a fork or comfortable branch and spend the night in it waiting for a shot at the marauder.

For weeks and sometimes months the strenuous hunt would go on in high tension up the hills and down the valleys as each new kill was reported, for every day gone meant more lives lost. Breakfasts, lunches and dinners were skipped. A man-eating tiger or leopard acquires a special cunning by its long association with humanity. It loses all fear, finding the biped the most defenceless creature in nature's kingdom. When this happens the hunter is also the hunted and gives himself at best a 50:50 chance in spite of his shooting iron. Corbett himself admits: 'There is no more terrible thing than to live and have one's being under the shadow of a maneater.'[3]

[3] *Man-Eaters of Kumaon,* p. 29.

2

A Sister Remembers

"Recollections of Jim Corbett" by Maggie Corbett, as Recounted to Ruby Beyts

Amongst the papers that D.C. Kala collected, while conducting research for his biography of Jim Corbett, are the personal reminiscences of Margaret Winifred Corbett. Better known as "Maggie", she was Jim's devoted sister and lifelong companion. Her account of his life was dictated in Kenya, after Jim's death, to her close friend Ruby Beyts, who was married to a retired Indian Army officer, Brigadier Geoffrey Herbert Bruno "Billy" Beyts. The typescript does not have a date but Maggie died in 1963 and it was probably recorded a year or two earlier.

Maggie was a constant presence in Corbett's life and makes regular appearance in his books, though he doesn't provide many details about her. In most cases she hovers in the background of his stories, helping him pack his bags before he sets off in pursuit of yet another man-eater, keeping house for him in Kaladhungi or Nainital, and helping him proofread the pages of his first publication, *Jungle Stories*. A variety of rumours and speculation surrounded this reclusive woman who was Corbett's closest friend and confidante. There are those who have suggested that she was actually the author of his books, though this is obviously false. Nevertheless, she was certainly his muse. Reading his letters to her, one can see that she was the first person to whom he recounted his shikar stories.

One of the most revealing aspects of Maggie's "Recollections" is the fact that she often accompanied Jim on his hunting and fishing trips – not the man-eater expeditions, but other forays into the jungle that involved less danger and discomfort. Her account of experiencing an earthquake in a boat, while fishing with Jim on Sattal lake, is a unique story that he never included in his publications. She also describes how he fell from a tree while trying to photograph a leopard and suffered near-fatal injuries, from which she nursed him back to health. In the midst of his long convalescence the chimney and roof of their home in Kaladhungi caught fire and Maggie helped put out the blaze while her brother lay immobilised in his bed. Anecdotes like this suggest that she was an equal partner in many of his adventures, supporting him but also taking an active part in his encounters with the natural world.

Both of Corbett's biographers, D.C. Kala and Martin Booth, have drawn from this document and quote parts of Ruby Beyts' typescript, but this is the first time it is being published in its entirety. Though hardly twenty pages in length, Maggie's reminiscences are full of details about the Corbett family, including her mother's two husbands, one of whom died during the 1857 uprising and the other of an apparent heart attack, while dressing for church. Altogether, they were a family of nine siblings, living off a life insurance policy for a while and then gradually acquiring property in Nainital. Mary Corbett, earlier Mary Doyle, was obviously a strong-willed and resourceful widow who struggled but succeeded in raising and educating her children. Towards the end of her life, Maggie and Jim lived with their mother at Gurney House and served as her caregivers. It was a convenient arrangement for all three of them and, when Mary died, Maggie and Jim continued to live together.

Recollections of Jim Corbett

As Told By His Sister Maggie to Ruby Beyts

~ JIM ~

Jim was always very proud of the fact that our family had been in India for so long, and for this reason I think it would be as well to begin his biography at the time of the arrival of our grandparents in India, at the beginning of the nineteenth century. They travelled from England in the days of sailing vessels, with the round voyage by the Cape of Good Hope taking about six months to accomplish, and the undertaking being quite an adventure.

Our Grandparents decided to remain in Calcutta, where they had landed, and it was not long before Grandfather found work there. First in a gun carriage factory at Ishapore, and later in a paper mill at Serampore. Three children – two sons and a daughter – were born to them. Grandfather died while still quite young, leaving his wife with the three children to bring up. When the boys were old enough to go to school, Grandmother decided to join her brother at Ferozepore in the Punjab, taking with her the little girl, Mary Jane, who was later to become our Mother. There were no railways at that time, and travelling was done by bullock cart and country boat. Nothing daunted, the two started off on a journey of many hundreds of miles without an escort, and after some months arrived safely at their destination, where they were warmly welcomed by our Grandunde and his family.

Our mother, while still very young, met a doctor by the name of Charles Doyle. They fell very much in love and were married when mother was fourteen (an age not considered at all unusual in those days), and her husband twenty one. The couple moved to Agra where four children were born to them: Charles, George, Eugene Mary and Evangeline. The last named died of small pox.

At the outbreak of the Indian Mutiny, Mother and her young children together with all the other women and children living in Agra, were moved into the Fort for safety, while the men fought the mutineers. Charles Doyle raised and commanded a mounted levy, was wounded twice and killed in action at Hurchandpur on December 8th, 1858. His horse was shot from under him, and he was cut to pieces. There is a memorial to him in the church at Etawah, near Agra, erected by his comrades, describing him as true hearted, generous, and gentle as he was brave.

Having been married for seven years and deeply devoted to her husband, Mother was now left with a small widow's pension, and three children to educate, but owing to her husband having taken out a Life Insurance Policy, she was able to use this money later on, to send Charles, George and Mary back to the United Kingdom for their training as doctors. Charles took his degree at Edinburgh and had a practice at Norwich. Later he went to America and settled in California, where he became a successful author, publishing several books, in particular "The Taming of the Jungle", and several volumes of poems.

George took his degree at Aberdeen, and then practiced at Heathfield in Sussex. Owing to ill health he was forced to give up his practice, and having been advised that sea air would be beneficial, he became a ship's doctor and sailed around the world three times, eventually returning to India where he practiced as a doctor till he died.

Eugene Mary (named after the Empress, for whom Charles Doyle had a great admiration), did her training to become a doctor partly in England and then in India. She worked for many years at St Catherine's Hospital in Amritsar. She was greatly beloved by the Indian population, as she used to travel round the villages giving medical aid, and could speak many dialects.

At the age of twenty three, Mother married for the second time, another doctor, Christopher William Corbett, our Father. He had taken part in the first Afghan War, the Sikh Wars of the eighteen forties, and had medals for the battles of Sobron, Allisal and Chillianwallah. He and his younger brother, Tom, also took part in the Indian Mutiny, during which Tom was tied to a tree and burnt alive in Delhi just as the relief force was arriving.

Father was a widower with two children when he married Mother, bringing their combined families up to five. In 1862, after having spent the first two years of their married life in Muttra and Mussoorie, Father, who had joined the Postal Service after the Mutiny, was transferred to Naini Tal.

As there was no train service the journey from Mussoorie to Naini Tal had to be made by "Doolie Dak". A Doolie was a large box like contrivance suspended from poles and capable of accommodating a number of people. This conveyance was carried on the shoulders of eight stalwart doolie bearers. Travelling by day as well as by night along a road, which ran for many miles through dense jungles teeming with wild life, the journey was not accomplished without its thrills. Sometimes the doolie had to be put down because of a tiger on the road, while strips would be torn from a bed sheet, soaked in kerosene oil, and used as flares to frighten the tiger away. The doolie would then continue on its journey. On arrival at Kaladungi, in the foot hills of the Himalayas, from where the road led steeply up to Nainital, a distance of fifteen miles over hills and valleys, the mode of travel was changed from the doolie to the dandy, a sort of hammock, composed of a durrie (a small cotton carpet) attached to a pole. This was placed on the ground and when the occupant was comfortably (?) settled in, and keeping uneasily in position by holding onto the pole, the journey was begun. It is hard to imagine a more uncomfortable method of travelling. Only women and children resorted to it. The men preferred to travel on horseback. Naini Tal, sacred to the Goddess Naini, and one of India's most beautiful hill stations, now became the home of our family, and it was here that Jim was born on July 25th 1875. Naini Tal at this time was a small settlement with a few houses dotted about on the hill sides, and a bazaar at each end of the lake. Our home was a single storey dwelling, with large airy rooms and a wide verandah on two sides looking towards the Cheena and Alma hills. The terraced garden, full of a profusion of flowers and shrubs was a mass of glorious colour, which was made even more beautiful by its lovely setting amidst the hills all around.

Our family increased until there were six boys and three girls; Thomas, Harriet, Christopher, John, Edith, Maurice, Margaret, Jim and Archibald. The Commissioner of Kumaon, Sir Henry Ramsay, to whom Jim refers in his book "Man Eaters of Kumaon", thought it would be a good idea for the family to have a place to go to during the winter, which was very severe in Naini Tal and very kindly gave Father a grant of land on which to build a house in Kaladungi.

Building materials were easy to find – stone from the nearby river beds, bricks burnt on the spot, and timber from the adjoining forest. Labour also was available and cheap, all the building along the foothills being done by the artisans from the hills who had come down to the low country to escape the cold. These people were known as the "Gham Taaps" – sun baskers – and formed the greater part of the winter foothill population. Our house, consisting of a big living room with bedrooms opening off it, and surrounded on three sides by a big verandah, became our winter home from the time of its completion. It stood on high ground in a lovely setting of bamboos and big trees. The plot was bounded on the East and West by dry river beds, and on the North by the Canal of which Jim writes in "Jungle Lore".

Father, who was a keen gardener, planted an orchard which was a source of great delight to us all with its variety of fruit.

In the year 1880 Naini Tal was devastated by a landslide which buried a big hotel and practically the whole of the shopping centre. The cause of the disaster was heavy and continuous rain lasting for three days and three nights, combined with a severe earthquake. The landslide, which came down in two portions, resulted in a very heavy death toll. All those who were buried under the debris when the second fall occurred were engaged in rescue work after the first fall of earth and rocks. Another cause for the great loss of life was that people were preparing their stalls for a fancy bazaar which was to take place that afternoon at the assembly rooms which were also carried away and buried. A friend of our mother was found crushed between two walls of the building.

There was at that time a military convalescent depot, at what was known as Kala Knau. The men from the depot were splendid in their rescue work, and a number of them were buried in the first fall of the landslide. An upper storey of one of the shops was lifted off bodily by the landslide and deposited intact on the playing field some distance in front of the building, and the dressmaker who was the only one to have stayed upstairs, while all the others including her young son out from school for the weekend had rushed downstairs in their panic, had escaped unhurt.

There is a beautiful memorial to all those who were killed, in the Church of St John in the Wilderness, Naini Tal. Sir William Willcocks, who later became famous for his irrigation work in Egypt, was invited to give expert advice on the drainage system of Naini, for it was considered that defective drainage had contributed towards the cause of the landslide.

For some while afterwards there was fear that a similar event might occur, and as a result my parents had to sell a large double-storey house they possessed at the time for a pittance, and they dismantled a smaller house in the same grounds, and moved the material to the opposite hillside. With this material they built the house that became our home.

On Easter Sunday in 1881, as Father was dressing to go to church, he became unwell and had to go to bed. His illness became worse and some weeks later he died and was buried in the cemetery of St John's Church. Some years later, the cemetery was closed. We have little recollection of Father as we were so young when he died, but from all we heard from Mother and those who knew him, we realised how much he was loved and respected by Indians and Europeans alike, who felt they could bring their joys and sorrows to him.

Mother was left with a number of young children to bring up and educate. A big responsibility, and had she not been as full of courage as she was, it would have been very hard for her. She seems to have shouldered her burden bravely. I have often thought that Jim inherited many of her characteristics; bravery, courage, generosity and kindliness combined with a high sense of duty. Although she never punished us, she expected implicit obedience from us, and I do not think she was disappointed. In appearance she was very small, with delicate features, lovely colouring and beautiful blue eyes. She was just the sort of mother to bring up boys. She did not fuss with them, and allowed them to follow their own natural bent in things that interested them. She was utterly unselfish and never felt that any self denial or self sacrifice on her part was too great, where her children were concerned, and how many thing she must have had to do without.

My half sister, Mary, was a great help to Mother in the education and general care of the younger children. A room in the house was set aside as a schoolroom, in which a school routine was observed with regular hours and a strict discipline. This was continued until we were old enough to go to school and to take our place with other children. Mary was musical and taught us to sing duets, and at times we would be called upon to perform before our elders. This we did, not at all enjoying the publicity, but we would not have thought of disobeying an elder sister. Jim had a very clear treble voice which later developed into a beautiful tenor.

We also learned to play a number of instruments. Jim on the guitar, the banjo and the flute, whilst I played the piano. We had a Shirmayer piano, a most beautiful instrument with a lovely tone. When we reached teen age, Mother would sometimes let us have a carpet dance in the big drawing room at Gurney House, and we would have great fun with our young friends. The girls took turns at playing the piano. We could dance most of the popular dances of the day: the Mazurka, Scottische, Polka, and the Square dances such as The Lancers, Roger de Coverly, Quadrilles etc.

Those were such happy days, and in fact we had a wonderfully happy childhood, although the strictest economy had to be observed and we did without many things which in this more luxurious age would be deemed necessities.

From the age of about nine or ten, Jim used to go off into the jungle for several days and nights at a stretch, accompanied by our gardener, an old and trusted family servant, as indeed all Indian servants were. They would light a fire at night to keep the tigers away, and during the day would observe the wild life and learn the way of the jungle. It was at this time that Jim began to imitate the calls of wild animals and birds. Although he never came to any harm, I can't help feeling Mother must have had some anxious moments, although she never showed any disquietude.

At a very early age Jim learned to use a catapult, the stones for which he carefully selected from among the nicely rounded ones in the river beds. He was a good shot from the beginning, and brought down many birds, of which there were a great variety of beautiful ones all along the foot hills. He learned to skin those he shot, and cured them very carefully, after which they were strung from a string which had been stretched across his bedroom for that purpose. He never just shot birds and threw them away. The catapult, in the course of time, gave way to a bow and pellets with which Jim became equally expert.

His constant companion was our young brother, Archie. The two boys were devoted to each other and there was a deep understanding between them. They enjoyed doing things together, and had the same love of sport and of all that is beautiful in Nature. Archie's admiration for Jim, his senior by four years, was unbounded, and I do not think there was ever a cross word spoken between the two boys, so great was their affection for each other.

The lake in Naini Tal afforded us the greatest pleasure, as with a "Ringhal" rod, thread and bent pin, we extracted many small fish from its deep waters. Jim soon began to catch bigger fish, and was once stopped by the Deputy Commissioner who told him jokingly that he would have to take out a licence if he were to catch such big fish. All through his life Jim loved fishing on the Naini lake, and often said he would rather fish there than anywhere else, even after he had fished in many parts of the world. He used the lightest tackle and would stand for hours in a boat, flyfishing. Some days we would start from home early enough to be at the further end of the lake by dawn, when Jim would begin fishing and continue until we caught sight of our man coming down the hill with a basket containing the early morning "chota hazri", consisting of tea and toast which Mary had prepared for us. The boat would then be drawn up to a quiet spot on the bank where we would enjoy the very welcome meal.

Jim started his school life at a private school of about sixty boys run by a man who was a harsh disciplinarian and used the cane very freely. Later Jim was removed from this school and sent to another larger establishment run by the American Methodist Mission, where he was very happy and soon became a favourite with masters and boys alike. He was never very fond of lessons nor the routine of school life, but he loved reading, and Fenimore Cooper was one of his favourite authors. At night in the dormitory he would read "The Pathfinder" or some other exciting book aloud to the other boys clustered around his bed.

From his earliest days Jim had a very real sense of responsibility, especially towards the family, and was ever conscious of its financial difficulties. As soon as he went out into the world and began to earn his living, he started to help financially with the education of Archie, even though this meant going without many necessities himself. He had never known anything different and as a boy at school his pocket money was only 4 annas a month.

Jim had no patience with self pity or anything that savoured of it. He always made the best of things and enjoyed life to the full. He never seemed hurried or flustered, but always found time to listen to the troubles of others. Never careless of his appearance, however shabby and old his clothes, he looked neat and tidy in them. Grace of movement, one of his most notable characteristics, was perhaps partly due to his having lived so much amongst wild animals, whose movements are always so graceful.

In 1906 Jim took over an engineering business from a friend who had become too old to carry on. With this business Jim also took over a large debt, under the burden of which he lived for some years. He tried to conduct this business whilst continuing his work at Mokameh Ghat. The strain of this proved too great, however as Naini Tal was separated from Mokameh Ghat by an enormous distance, so in 1909 Mary and I took over the engineering business, and with the help of an Indian and staff managed to run it for ten years.

In 1917 Jim purchased the village of Chota Haldwani in Kaladungi. The place was practically derelict with most of the houses in ruins and the fields completely overgrown with grass and weeds.

He very soon set to work to remedy this sorry state of affairs by fencing in the village, little by little as his means permitted and later substituting the wire fence with a masonry wall 5 ft. 10″ high. Jim personally assisted in the clearing of the land spending many hours cutting bush and moving heavy rocks.

Later he built a cement water way, thereby replacing the old rough channel through which there had been so much seepage that the lower end of the village received only a small trickle of water, quite inadequate for its many needs.

In the surrounding boundary walls gates were made, to provide the villagers with easy entrances and exits for their cattle and carts. As means permitted, Jim had new houses built and old houses renovated. News of all this renovation quickly spread, and people soon came forward to take up land, and gradually the village developed into one of the best in that part of the country.

Often as I walked along its paths as the sun went down with the evening light on the ripening corn and the blue hills in the background, I would think there could not be a more beautiful village in the world. To make conditions easier for his tenants, Jim paid the Government Revenue for them and continued to do so as long as he lived. He encouraged the villagers to grow their own fruit and vegetables, not only so that they should have a more varied diet, but also that they should be able to sell their surplus in the market. From his estate in Tanganyika, which I mention later, Jim brought banana plants of the best varieties and from the Botanical Gardens in Saharanpur he brought grape vines and fruit trees.

Apart from all that Jim did to help his tenants in Choti Haldwani, he also encouraged the inhabitants in the district to grow better maize. This he did by distributing a cigarette tin full of seed, which he had brought from Tanganyika, to each man and woman as they came to do their business in the Naini Tal market. The people were anxious to have the seed in order to grow bigger and better "Bhutas" than ever before, and soon produced maize cobs as much as fourteen inches long in place of the very ordinary ones they had been growing up to this time.

The villagers from far and wide came to Jim for medical aid, and had the utmost confidence in his treatment. Malarial cases were the most frequent, and their constitutions were so weakened by this scourge, that during the winter months they were unable to stand up to the cold, with the result that they developed pneumonia and all sorts of bronchial trouble. A common cause of earache came from a tick making its way into the inner ear. This was easily cured by inserting a few drops of olive oil into the affected part. Women often came with bad injuries caused by falling from high branches of trees, whilst cutting leaves with which they fed their cattle. There were also cases of dog bite, and on one occasion a woman had the muscles of her leg torn out while separating two cats who were fighting. There were two cement platforms under a big mango tree in the garden, which formed the surgery, and on these platforms the patients were treated.

When the time came for Jim to return to Naini Tal, the people would say, "What are we to do while you are away?" Jim would then tell them of simple remedies, such as a hot lemon and honey drink for a cold, or a poultice of wholemeal for a boil etc. All the villagers of Kumaon loved and respected Jim for his kindness and his humanity.

Each year at Christmas we had a village treat, supposedly for the children of our village. But there was no age limit, and there would be babies in arms, young men and women, and grey haired grand parents. Others in the outlying villages soon got to hear of the annual entertainment, and began to join in, until the numbers increased to hundreds, and all were welcome.

The treat was timed to start at 3 pm but long before that, on the great day, from early in the morning a steady trickle of guests started to arrive. Attired in their best and gayest apparel, they were content to wait, chattering and laughing with their friends until zero hour arrived.

The school children in charge of a master would line up in front of the house and shout "Garge Panchim Badshah ki Jai" followed by "Corbett Sahib ki Jai", and then march off in a neat line to the nearby field where the entertainment was due to take place. The party commenced with all our guests sitting on the ground in an enormous ring, and our men – who had to be of very high caste – would then go round with big baskets distributing sweets. These had been especially ordered from the bazaar, and the Bania had been up at dawn preparing them as Indian sweets have to be absolutely fresh to be worth eating. After the sweets, fruit would go round, oranges and bananas being chief favourites.

The feast over, games began and these were many and varied. People of all ages took part. I think the game the children enjoyed most of all was that in which a blindfold child had to pierce with a stick a paper bag filled to the brim with sweets, and suspended from a horizontal pole. The fun continued until the sun began to sink low in the West, when after many expressions of gratitude for such a lovely day, everyone would return home, tired but happy. The village people had so few pleasures that they appreciated to the full a simple entertainment such as this, and it afforded them much to talk over and laugh about during their leisure hours.

In the autumn of 1915 Kumaon experienced a very severe earthquake – the most horrifying that we had ever known. Jim and I were in a boat fishing on the Sath Tal lake, about twelve miles from Naini Tal. Suddenly the boat began to quiver in a most unaccountable way, and the first thought that flashed across my mind was that the quivering was due to a volcanic eruption. The Kumaon lakes were thought to have been formed in this way. The quivering rapidly increased becoming more and more violent until I thought the boat must be upset. The fish being alarmed by the disturbance in the water, were jumping upon all sides, and a huge snake went swimming across the lake at a great speed. At the same time there was a tremendous report and rocks came crashing down the hillside bringing enormous trees in their wake. All this was very alarming and I suggested we might get off the water, but Jim said we were safer where we were. After a while the noise and disturbance ceased and all was quiet once more. A few days after, Jim happened to be passing through some villages of Kumaon, where he found that numbers of houses had collapsed and were in ruins due to the earthquake.

Jim's next experience of an earthquake was when he was sitting up in a tree in Kaladungi, hoping to get a picture of a leopard. Suddenly the tree in which he was perched began to wave about, and Jim wondered whether it was the leopard trying to get at him from behind or whether it was a big snake crawling up the tree. On looking around, however, he saw the other trees behaving in a similar manner, although there was no wind, and later he discovered that this was the tail end of the disastrous Bihar earthquake in which thousands of people perished.

Another day as we were crossing the Bole Briar,[1] on our way home from an evening walk in the jungle, the creaking of the metal bridge told us that an earthquake was in progress. This

[1] The meaning here is unclear but she likely meant the Bore Bridge.

was not severe, however, and we just stood where we were whilst the shock lasted.

Jim was very fond of photographing the animals in the jungle, and early one afternoon he set off hoping to get a picture of a tiger which he knew was in the jungle just beyond the canal. Before he went, he told me to expect him back in time for tea. Some friends who were expected for tea duly arrived, and time went on as we sat chatting. The sun went down and I began to feel anxious as there was no sign of Jim. As darkness fell my anxiety increased, and I wondered whether or not to institute a search party. But knowing how much Jim hated me to worry about him I hesitated to do this. The hours dragged by, when suddenly there was the sound of voices, a white face appeared at the window, the door was opened and Jim appeared supported by the two men who had accompanied him. Barely able to stand, Jim collapsed on the sofa, obviously in great pain and hardly aware of what he was doing or saying. I at once realised there was something seriously wrong, when Jim, who was never in the habit of drinking alcohol, asked for a whisky, which when brought he drank at a gulp. When I asked him what had happened, Jim replied that he thought he had fallen from the aqueduct on the way home. This was not so, however. The two men who were with him told me that according to Jim's instructions, they were waiting some way off from the tree in which Jim was sitting with his camera. After some hours when there was obviously no hope of photography in the fading light, they saw Jim let down his camera by a string from the tree, and then they heard a great cry, and on running to the spot found Jim lying at the foot of the tree unable to move. (Afterwards Jim was never able to account for his fall.) They lifted him up and supporting him on their shoulders, managed to bring him home.

I had a bed brought into the drawing room for Jim, as he was in such great pain, and after a terrible night, I set off in the early morning to go to the Rest Bungalow, to ask some friends who were staying there for a few days, to telephone for the doctor. This they did and after some hours the doctor arrived. On examination Jim was found to have a broken back, severe concussion, and internal haemorrhage. As he was too ill to be moved to hospital the doctor strapped round and round with strapping, and we nursed him day and night. After some months owing to Jim's amazing resilience, he recovered. Early one morning during this illness I had gone into Jim's room to take him some tea, when I saw to my horror flames roaring up the chimney and found they had set the roof ablaze. Jim told me to get a blanket quickly, soak it in water and hold it in front of the fire. In my haste I took a beautiful rug which Jim had bought for me at an exhibition, immersed it in the bath, and pushed it up the flue. By this time men were on the roof, removing the chimney capital and burning timbers. Gallons of water were cascading down into the room, and there was Jim lying in his bed in the middle of a flood.

I was in the habit of taking the dogs out in the garden for a little run after breakfast. One morning, a white eagle came sailing down out of the blue sky and alighted amongst the dogs, who were not in the least perturbed by this unexpected visitor. We continued with our walk and the eagle came with us. Thereafter it often joined us in the garden, and later took to walking about on the verandah where Jim was convalescing, on a sofa, and would drink from a bowl of water set there for the dogs. This was one of a pair of eagles that we had seen about the place for some time, and who were still there when we returned to Kaladungi the following winter. But the friendly bird did not return to us again.

In 1922 Mr Wyndham, who was the Commissioner of Kumaon, and a personal friend, suggested to Jim that they should go together to Tanganyika where Mr Wyndham had a coffee farm at Kikafu on the slopes of Mt Kilimanjaro. Jim was so taken with the place that when Mr Wyndham suggested they become partners, Jim eagerly agreed. He built a house there of which he was very proud, as he laid most of the brick himself.

Owing to their commitments in India neither Jim nor Mr Wyndham could remain in Tanganyika for many months at a time, so Major Bellairs who had been a tea planter in India, joined the Kikafu Estate and managed it until 1947 when the Government bought it from them. During this period Jim went over annually for 14 years, and it was then he told me that when the time came for him to retire it would be to one of the silent places of the earth.

In December 1947 after Independence came to India and our British friends were leaving, we began to realise that it would be very difficult for us to remain, especially as when the time came for one of us to be taken, the contemplation of the other having to live on alone in Gurney House, our home for nearly all the years of our lives and so full of memories, could not be faced.

We therefore decided very reluctantly to leave. Our choice of destination fell on Kenya, the reason being that Jim knew the country, and we felt the conditions of life there would be much like those we had been used to in India. Jim had a very serious illness the last year we were in India. We had been on a fishing trip to the Kosi and Ramganga – two very big rivers in Kumaon – and while there Jim was suddenly taken ill with a very high temperature and had to be taken to the Ramsey Hospital where he was found to be suffering from both benign and malignant malaria. After a day or two in the hospital he also developed pneumonia and was so ill that the doctors despaired of his life. However with careful and efficient nursing he gradually improved and was able to leave hospital in about a month.

Not long after this we had to begin making preparations for the move to Kenya. The morning we were due to leave, we looked across the waters of the lake which was indescribably beautiful in the early morning light. Our servants did not help make our departure any easier as they stood with tears trickling down their cheeks as we moved down the hill from the house we knew we should never see again. Accommodation in Bombay at that time was very difficult to find as so many Britons were leaving, and all hotels were fully booked. We were, however, very fortunate in having a friend who put us up in his beautiful flat overlooking the sea, while we waited for our ship to sail.

We arrived in Kenya on December 15th 1947, and after a short time with friends near Nairobi, we came to the Outspan Hotel in Nyeri and lived in Lord Baden Powell's cottage, which continued to be our home until the time of Jim's death in April 1955.

We lived very happily in this charming cottage and gradually made the garden into a small bird sanctuary. Some of the birds became so tame as to feed out of our hands. Jim counted twenty six varieties of birds, attracted not only by the food we gave them but also by a lovely little pond at the foot of the verandah steps in which they could bathe. We had several kinds of weavers, besides robins, thrushes, glossy starlings and white eyes, these last being the most responsive of all, coming to the call of a whistle. The tiny cardinal wax bills are perhaps the most confiding of all, picking up at our feet the crumbs dropped by other birds.

It was here in this peaceful spot within sight of Mt Kenya that Jim wrote all his books with the exception of "Man-eaters of Kumaon", and a small book of Jungle Stories of which he had had only one hundred copies printed by a small printing press in Naini Tal to give to friends.

Soon after his arrival in India as Viceroy, Lord Linlithgow, whilst on a visit to the Governor of the United Provinces, was lent a copy of this little book and was so interested in it that he expressed a wish to possess a copy for himself. This wish was conveyed to Jim who sent Lord Linlithgow a copy. I think it was the reading of this little book that led to the Viceroy's desire to visit the scene of some of the stories, for in the following spring Jim received a message from one of the Viceregal staff asking if we could suggest a place in which the Viceroy could spend a holiday and get some shooting. Jim suggested Kaladungi and we were greatly honoured by an invitation to house Lord and Lady Linlithgow on several occasions and also to visit them in Simla. He very much enjoyed this visit. Jim especially enjoyed his games of tennis and billiards with Lord Linlithgow. During our visit the Maharaja of Patiala invited the Viceregal Party to a very enjoyable bird shoot in his State. Later on we were invited to the Viceroy's house in Delhi. The last occasion was a farewell visit on the eve of Lord and Lady Linlithgow's departure from India.

Jim's cine photography was a great delight to him and he would take infinite pains to get the best results. He always went unarmed to take his jungle pictures. I felt he was taking risks in so doing, especially during the time he spent in filming the seven tigers he had managed to get together. He always sat in the same place, about eight feet from the ground on the branch of a very small tree under which the tigers had to pass on the way to the place where they fed. So as not to disturb them, Jim took up his position very early in the morning. By putting out his hand he could have touched the tigers on their backs as they passed below him.

Jim never kept well in Nyeri. The pneumonia had left him with adhesions in his lungs which made breathing difficult more particularly owing to the lack of oxygen in the air and volcanic dust which one breathed constantly especially during the dry season. Jim was in hospital two or three times with bronchitis and after each attack his breathing became more difficult. I used sometimes to feel that we should not continue to live in Nyeri, but Jim would say, "One has to live somewhere." He gradually lost ground and grew very weak. His thoughts to the last were always for others, and the last words he spoke to me were "Always be brave, and try and make the world a happier place for others to live in."

Jim's heart always remained in the jungles and hills of Kumaon, and I am sure he will never be forgotten by the Indian people whom he loved so much.

3

Jim Corbett's First Book

Jungle Stories

For a flimsy paperbound booklet published in 1935, one of the few surviving copies of Jim Corbett's *Jungle Stories* is in remarkably good condition. It was obviously a prized possession and well cared for by its original owner, who wrapped it in a plastic dust jacket. No photograph of a snarling tiger decorates the cover, which consists of dull brown paper with the title printed at the centre and the author's name in the lower right hand corner. Neither decorations nor endorsements embellish this slender volume. It is as self-effacing and ascetic in appearance as the man who wrote the seven pieces that fill the book's 104 pages.

At several points in the text, Corbett refers to photographs that he intended to include as illustrations, though these seem not to have found their way into the publication. The book was produced on a shoestring budget and, as Corbett describes it, the printing process at the London Press in Nainital was makeshift and laborious:

> When I had copied them, I took the stories to a friend who had a small hand printing press. He had never before printed books, but being a good friend, he undertook the job. His stock type was, however, so limited that he was only able to print one page at a time and, after my sister and I had made what corrections were necessary, he printed off a hundred copies. The type was then broken up and set for the next page. In this way, he took four months to print the book which we called 'Jungle Stories'. I retained one copy and then I started distributing the other copies to friends. But owing to demands for additional copies for relatives in other parts of the world, I was only able to give seventy-five friends

> copies. These copies drifted from hand to hand until the majority had been read to death.[1]

Jungle Stories eventually found its way into the hands of the Viceroy of India, Lord Linlithgow, who was an avid hunter. He enjoyed the book and recommended it to the Oxford University Press, where a young editor named R.E. Hawkins picked it up and gently but expertly guided Jim Corbett into expanding the table of contents by adding six more shikar stories. Eventually, because of a delay caused by World War II, OUP published *Man-Eaters of Kumaon* in 1944. Four of the chapters from *Jungle Stories* found their way into that book – "The Pipal Pani Tiger", "Fish of My Dreams", "The Terror that Walks by Night" (renamed "The Kanda Man-eater"), and "The Chowgarh Tigers". Of the remaining three chapters, a version of "Purna Giri and its Mysterious Lights" appears in *The Temple Tiger and More Man-Eaters of Kumaon* (1954). "Wildlife in the Village: An Appeal" was included in an anthology edited by Hawkins, *Jim Corbett's India* (1978). To the best of our knowledge, "A Lost Paradise" has not appeared in print since the first edition. Of course, *Man-Eaters of Kumaon* went on to become an international bestseller and, at last count, more than four million copies have been sold.

While most of this self-published book will be familiar to Corbett's loyal readers, it is interesting to see the way in which the content and structure of the stories, as well as the author's voice, remain largely unchanged. R.E. Hawkins had a very light

[1] Jim Corbett, *My Kumaon: Uncollected Writings* (Delhi: Oxford University Press, 2012), pp. xv–xvi.

touch as an editor and he seems to have suggested only minor corrections. Corbett used the archaic "shewed", which OUP changed to "showed", and some of the longer paragraphs were broken up to give his lengthy descriptions some breathing space. Other than that, the hand-set type in the first printing of a hundred copies is no different from what appears in dozens of other editions of the book that made Jim Corbett famous. If anything, a comparison between the four chapters in *Jungle Stories* and their later renditions in *Man-Eaters of Kumaon* will prove that, from the start, Corbett's skills as a writer were equal to his accomplishments as a hunter and naturalist.

Jungle Stories

By Jim Corbett

Dedicated to the hundreds of men, women and children of Kumaon, killed by the man-eaters of: —

Champawat

Muktesar

Panar

Rudra Prayag

Talla Des. (3)

Chowgarh (2)

Mohan

Kanda

CONTENTS

*These page numbers refer to those in the original edition.

THE PIPAL PANI TIGER

Beyond the fact that he was born in a ravine running deep into the foot hills and was one of a family of three, I know nothing of his early history.

He was about a year old when, attracted by the calling of a cheetle hind early one November morning, I found his pug marks in the sandy bed of a little stream known locally as "Pipal Pani". I thought at first that he had strayed from his mother's care but, as week succeeded week and his single tracks showed on the game paths of the forest, I came to the conclusion that the near approach of the breeding season was an all sufficient reason for his being alone. Jealously guarded one day, protected at the cost of the parent life if necessary, and set adrift the next, is the lot of all jungle folk; nature's method of preventing inbreeding.

That winter he lived on peafowl, karker, small pig and an occasional cheetle hind, making his home in a prostrate giant of the forest felled for no apparent reason, and hollowed out by time and porcupines. Here he brought most of his kills, basking, when the days were cold, on the smooth bole of the tree, where many a leopard had basked before him.

It was not until January was well advanced that I saw the cub at close quarters. I was out one evening without any definite object in view, when I saw a crow rise from the ground and wipe its beak as it lit on the branch of a tree. Crows, vultures and magpies always interest me in the jungle, and many are the kills I have found both in India and Africa with the help of these birds. On the present occasion the crow led me to the scene of an overnight tragedy. A cheetle had been killed and partly eaten and, attracted to the spot probably as I had been, a party of men passing along the road distant some fifty yards, had cut up and removed the remains. All that was left of the cheetle were a few splinters of bone, and a little congealed blood off which the crow had lately made his meal. The absence of thick cover and the proximity of the road convinced me the animal responsible for the kill had not witnessed the removal and that it would return in due course; so I decided to sit up, and made myself as comfortable in a plum tree as the thorns permitted.

I make no apology to you, my reader, if you differ with me on the ethics of the much debated subject of sitting up over kills. Some of my most pleasant shikar memories centre round the hour or two before sunset that I have spent in a tree over a natural kill, ranging from the time when armed with a muzzle loader, whipped round with brass wire to prevent the cracked barrel from bursting, I sat over a langoor killed by a leopard, to a few days ago, when armed with the most modern rifle across my knees, I watched a tigress and her two full grown cubs eat up a sambhar stag they had killed, and counted myself no poorer for not having taken a trophy.

True, on the present occasion there is no kill below me but, for the reasons given, that will not affect my chance of a shot; scent to interest the jungle folk there is in plenty in the blood-soaked ground, as witness the old grey whiskered boar who has been quietly rooting along for the past ten minutes, and who suddenly stiffens to attention as he comes into the line of the blood tainted wind. His snout held high, and worked as only a pig can work that member, tells him more than I was able to glean from the ground which showed no tracks; his method of approach, a short excursion to the right and back into the wind, and then a short excursion to the left and again back into the wind, each manoeuvre bringing him a few yards nearer, indicates the cheetle was killed by a tiger. Making sure once and again that nothing worth eating has been left, he finally trots off and disappears from view.

Two cheetle, both with horns in velvet, now appear and from the fact that they are coming down wind, and making straight for the blood-soaked spot, it is evident they were witness to the overnight tragedy. Alternately snuffing the ground, or standing rigid with every muscle tensed for instant flight, they satisfy their curiosity and return the way they came.

Curiosity is not a human monopoly, and many an animal's life is cut short by indulging in it. A dog leaves the verandah to bark at a shadow, a deer leaves the herd to investigate a tuft of grass that no wind agitated, and the waiting leopard is provided with a meal.

The sun is nearing the winter line when a movement to the right front attracts attention. An animal has crossed an opening between two bushes at the far end of a wedge of scrub that terminates thirty yards from my tree. Presently the bushes at my end part and out into the open, with never a look to right or left, steps the cub. Straight up to the spot where his kill had been, he goes, his look of expectancy giving place to one of disappointment as he realises that his cheetle killed, possibly after hours of patient stalking, is gone. The splinters of bone and congealed blood are rejected, and his interest centres on a tree stump lately used as a butcher's block to which some shreds of flesh are adhering. I was not the only one who carried fire arms in those jungles and, if the cub was to grow into a tiger, it was necessary he should be taught the danger of carelessly approaching kills in day-light. A scatter gun and dust shot would have served my purpose better, but the rifle will have to do this time and, as he raised his head to smell the stump, my bullet crashed into the hard wood an inch from his nose. Only once in the years that followed did the cub forget that lesson.

The following winter I saw him several times. His ears did not look so big now and he had changed his baby hair for a coat of rich tawny red with well defined stripes. The hollow tree had been given up to its rightful owners, a pair of leopards, new quarters found in a thick belt of scrub skirting the foot hills, and young sambhar added to his menu.

On my annual descent from the hills next winter, the familiar pug marks no longer showed on the game paths and at the drinking places, and for several weeks I thought the cub had abandoned his old haunts and gone further afield. Then one morning his absence was explained for, side by side with his tracks, were the smaller and more elongated tracks of the mate he had gone to find. I only once saw the tigers, for the cub was a tiger now, together. I had been out before dawn to try and bag a serow that lived on the foot hills, and returning along a fire track my attention was arrested by a vulture, perched on the dead limb of a sal tree. The bird had his back towards me and was facing a short stretch of scrub with dense jungle beyond. Dew was still heavy on the ground and, without a sound I reached the tree, and peered round. One antler of a dead sambhar, for no living deer would lie in that position, projected above the low bushes. A convenient moss-covered rock afforded my rubber-shod feet silent and safe hold, and as I drew myself erect, the sambhar came into full view. The hindquarters had been eaten away and, lying on either side of the kill, were the tigers, the tiger being on the far side with only his hind legs showing; both tigers were asleep. Ten feet straight in front, to avoid a dead branch and thirty feet to the left would give me a shot at the tiger's neck, but in planning the stalk I had forgotten the silent spectator. Where I stood I was invisible to him, but before the ten feet had been covered I came into view and, alarmed at my near proximity, he flapped off his perch, omitting as he did so to note a thin creeper dependent from a branch above him against which he collided coming ignominiously to ground. The tigress was up and away in an instant, clearing at a bound the kill and her mate, the tiger not being slow to follow; a possible shot, but too risky with thick jungle ahead where a wounded animal would have all the advantages. To those who have never tried it, I can recommend the stalking of leopards and tigers on their kills as a most pleasant form of sport. Great care should be taken over the shot, for if the animal is not killed outright or anchored, trouble is bound to follow.

A week later the tiger resumed his bachelor existence. A change had now come over his nature. Hitherto he had not objected to my visiting his kill but, after his mate left, at the first drag I followed up, I was given very clearly to understand that no liberties would in future be permitted. The angry growl of a tiger at close quarters, than which there is no more terrifying sound in the jungle has to be heard to be appreciated.

Early in March the tiger killed his first full grown buffalo. I was near the foot hills one evening when the agonised bellowing of a buffalo, mingled with the angry roar of a tiger, rang through the forest. I located the sounds as coming from a ravine about six hundred yards away. The going was bad, mostly over loose rocks and through thorn bushes and when I crawled up a steep bluff commanding a view of the ravine, the buffalo's struggles were over, and the tiger nowhere to be seen. For an hour I lay with finger on trigger without seeing anything of the tiger. At dawn next morning I again crawled up the bluff, to find the buffalo lying as I had left her. The soft ground, torn by hoof and claw, testified to the desperate nature of the struggle, and it was not until the buffalo had been hamstrung that the tiger had finally succeeded in pulling her down in a fight which had lasted from ten to fifteen minutes. The tiger's tracks led across the ravine and, on following them up, I found a long smear of blood on a rock and, a hundred yards further on, another smear on a fallen tree. The wound inflicted by the buffalo's horns was in the head and sufficiently severe to make the tiger lose all interest in the kill, for he never returned to it.

Three years later the tiger, disregarding the lesson received when a cub (his excuse may have been that it was the close season for tigers), incautiously returned to a kill, over which a zamindar and some of his tenants were sitting at night, and received a bullet in the shoulder which fractured the bone. No attempt was made to follow him up, and thirty six hours later, his shoulder covered with a swarm of flies, he limped through the compound of the inspection bungalow, crossed a bridge flanked on the far side by a double row of tenanted houses, the occupants of which stood at their doors to watch him pass, entered the gate of a walled-in compound and took possession of a vacant godown. Twenty-four hours later, possibly alarmed by the number of people who had collected from surrounding villages to see him, he left the compound the way he had entered it, passed my gate, and made his painful way to the lower end of the village. A bullock belonging to one of my tenants had died the previous night and had been dragged into some bushes at the edge of the village; this the tiger found, and here he remained a few days, quenching his thirst at an irrigation furrow.

When I came down from the hills two months later the tiger was living on small animals (calves, sheep, goats, etc.) that he was able to catch on the outskirts of the village. By March his wound had healed leaving his right foot turned inwards. Returning to the forest where he had been wounded, he levied heavy toll on the village cattle taking, for safety sake, but one meal off each and in this way killing five times as many as he would ordinarily have done. The zamindar who had wounded him and who had a herd of some four hundred head of cows and buffaloes, was the chief sufferer.

In the succeeding year he gained as much in size as in reputation and many were the attempts made by sportsmen, and others, to bag him.

One November evening, a villager, armed with a single barrel muzzle loader, set out to try and bag a pig, selecting for his *patwa* or ground *machan* an isolated bush growing in a twenty yard wide *rowkhar* (dry water course) running down the centre of some five acres of broken ground. This ground was rectangular, flanked on the long sides by cultivated land and on the short sides by a road, and a ten foot wide canal that formed the boundary between the cultivated land and the forest. In front of the man was a four-foot bank with a cattle track along the upper edge; behind him a patch of heavy scrub. At 8 p.m. an animal appeared on the track and, taking what aim he could, he fired. On receiving the shot the animal fell off the bank and passed within a few feet of the man, grunting as it entered the scrub behind. Casting aside his blanket, the man ran to his hut two hundred yards away. Neighbours soon collected and, on hearing the man's account, came to the conclusion that a pig had been hard hit. It would be a pity to leave the pig for hyaenas and jackals to eat, so a lantern was lit and, as a party of six bold spirits set out to retrieve the bag, a man who declined to join the expedition and who confessed to me later that he had no stomach for looking for wounded pig in the dark, suggested that the gun should be taken.

His suggestion was accepted and, as a liberal charge of powder was being rammed home, the ramrod jammed and broke inside the barrel. A trivial accident which undoubtedly saved the lives of six men. The broken rod eventually and after great trouble, extracted and the gun loaded, the party set off.

Arrived at the spot where the animal had entered the bushes, a careful search was made and, on blood being found, every effort to find the pig was made; it was not until the whole area had been combed out that the quest for that night was finally abandoned. Early next morning the search was resumed, with the addition of my informant of weak stomach, who was a better woodsman than his companions and who, on examining the ground under a bush where there was a lot of blood, collected some hairs which he brought to me. A brother sportsman was with me for the day and together we went to have a look at the ground.

The reconstruction of jungle events from signs on the ground has always held great interest for me. True one's deductions are sometimes wrong, but they are also sometimes right. In the present instance I was right in placing the wound in the inner forearm of the right foreleg but was wrong in assuming the leg had been broken and that the tiger was a young animal and a stranger to the locality.

There was no blood beyond the point where the hairs had been found and, as tracking on the hard ground was impossible, I crossed the canal to where the cattle track ran through a bed of sand. Here from the pug marks I found that the wounded animal was not a young tiger as I had assumed, but my old friend the Pipal Pani tiger who, when taking a short cut through the village, had in the dark been mistaken for a pig.

Once before when badly wounded he had passed through the settlement without harming man or beast but he was older now and, if driven by pain and hunger, might do considerable damage. A disconcerting prospect, for the locality was thickly populated, and I was due to leave within the week, to keep an engagement that could not be put off.

For three days I searched every bit of the jungle between the canal and the foot hills, an area of about four square miles, without finding any trace of the tiger. On the fourth afternoon, as I was setting out to continue the search, I met an old woman and her son hurriedly leaving the jungle. From them I learnt that the tiger was calling near the foot hills and that all the cattle feeding in the jungle had stampeded. When out with a rifle, I invariably go alone; it's safer in a mix up and one can get through the jungle more silently. However, I stretched a point on this occasion, and let the boy accompany me since he was very keen on showing me where he had heard the tiger.

Arrived at the foot hills, the boy pointed to a fire track to which I have already referred, and on the near side by the Pipal Pani stream. Running parallel to, and about a hundred yards from the stream was a shallow depression some twenty feet wide, more or less open on one side and fringed with bushes on the side nearer the stream. A well used foot path crossed the depression at right angles. Twenty yards from the path, and on the open side of the depression was a small tree. If the tiger came down the path he would in all likelihood stand for a shot on clearing the bushes. Here I decided to take my stand and, putting the boy into the tree with his feet on a level with my head and instructing him to signal with his toes if, from his raised position, he saw the tiger before I did, I put my back to the tree and called.

You, who have spent as many years in the forest as I have, need no description of the call of a tigress in search of a mate, and to you less fortunate ones I can only say that the call, to acquire which necessitates years of close observation and the liberal use of throat salve, cannot be described in words.

To my great relief, for I had crawled through the forest for three full days with finger on trigger, I was immediately answered from a distance of about five hundred yards, and for half an hour thereafter – it may have been a little less and certainly appeared much more – the call was tossed back and forth. On the one side the urgent summon of the King, and on the other, the subdued and coaxing answer of his handmaiden. Twice the boy signalled, but I had as yet seen nothing of the tiger and it was not until the setting sun was flooding the forest with golden light that he suddenly appeared, coming down the path at a fast walk with never a pause as he cleared the bushes. When half way across the depression and just as I was raising the rifle, he turned to the right and came straight toward me.

This manoeuvre, unforeseen when selecting my stand, brought him nearer than I had intended he should come and, moreover, presented me with a head shot which at that short range, I was not prepared to take. Resorting to an old device, learned years ago and successfully used on similar occasions, the tiger was brought to a stand without being alarmed. With one paw poised, he slowly raised his head, exposing chest and throat. Struggling to his feet after impact of the heavy bullet he tore blindly through the forest, coming down with a crash within a few yards of where, attracted by the calling of a cheetle hind one November morning, I had first seen his pug marks. It was only then that I found he had been shot under a misapprehension, for the wound, which I feared might make him dangerous, proved on examination to be almost healed and caused by a pellet of lead having severed a small vein in his right forearm.

Pleasure at having secured a magnificent trophy (10′-3″) was not unmixed with regret, for never again would the jungle-folk and I listen with held breath to his deep throated roar, resounding through the foot hills, and never again would his familiar pug marks show on the game paths we had trodden for fifteen years.

THE FISH OF MY DREAMS

Fishing for mahseer in a well stocked submontane river is, in my opinion, the most fascinating of all field sports. Our environments, even though we may not be continuously conscious of them, nevertheless play a very important part in the sum total of our enjoyment of any form of outdoor sport. I am convinced that the killing of the fish of one's dreams in uncongenial surroundings would afford an angler as little pleasure, as the winning of the Davis Cup would to a tennis player if the contest were staged in the Sahara.

The river I have recently been fishing in, flows for some forty miles of its length, through a beautifully wooded valley, well stocked with game and teeming with bird life. I had the curiosity to count the various kinds of animals and birds seen in one day, and by evening of that day my count showed among animals, sambhar, cheetal, karkar, ghooral, pig, langoor and red monkeys, and among birds, seventy-five varieties, including peafowl, red jungle fowl, kaleg pheasants, black partridge and bush quail.

In addition to these I saw a school of five otter in the river, several small mugger and a python. The python was lying on the surface of a big still pool, with only the top of its flat head and eyes projecting above the gin-clear water. The subject was one I had long wished to photograph, and in order to do this it was necessary to cross the river above the pool, and climb the opposite hillside, but unfortunately I had been seen, and as I cautiously stepped backwards, the reptile, which appeared to be about 18 feet long, submerged, to retire to its subterranean home, among the piled up boulders at the head of the pool.

In some places the valley through which the river flows, is so narrow that a stone can be tossed with ease from one side to the other, and in other places, widens out to a mile or more. In these open spaces grow amaltas with their two feet long sprays of golden bloom, karaunda and box bushes with their white star-shaped flowers, the combined scent from these flowers filling the air, which throbs with the spring songs of a multitude of birds, with the most delicate and pleasing of perfumes. In these environments, angling for mahseer might well be described as sport fit for kings. My object in visiting this sportsman's paradise was not, however, to kill mahseer, but to try and secure a day-light picture of a tiger, and it was only when light conditions were unfavourable, that I laid aside my camera for a rod.

I had been out from dawn one day, trying hour after hour, to get a picture of a tigress and her two cubs. The tigress was a young animal, nervous as all young mothers are, and as often as I stalked her, she retired with the cubs into heavy cover. There is a limit to the disturbance a tigress, be she young or old, will suffer when accompanied by cubs and when the limit on this occasion had been reached, I altered my tactics and tried sitting up in trees over open glades, and lying in high grass near a stagnant pool, in which she and her family were accustomed to drink, but with no better success.

When the declining sun was beginning to cast shadows over the open places I was watching, I gave up the attempt, and added the day to the several hundred days I had already spent, in trying to get a picture of a tiger in its natural surrounding. The two men I had brought from camp, had passed the day in the shade of a tree on the far side of the river. Calling them up I instructed them to return to camp by way of the forest track, and exchanging my camera for a rod, I set off alone along the river, intent on catching a fish for my dinner.

The fashion in rods and tackle has altered, in recent years, as much as the fashion in ladies' dress. Gone, one often wonders where, are the 18-foot green heart rods with their unbreakable accompaniments and gone the muscles needed to wield them, and their place has been taken by light one-handed fly rods.

I was armed with an 11-foot tournament trout rod, a reel containing 50 yards of casting line and 200 yards of silk backing, a medium gut cast and a one-in home-made brass spoon.

When one has unlimited undisturbed water to fish, one is apt to be over-critical. A pool is discarded because the approach to it is over rough ground, or a run is rejected because of a suspected snag. On this occasion, half-a-mile had been traversed before a final selection was made. A welter of white water cascading over rocks at the head of a deep oily run 80 yards long, and at the end of the run a deep still pool 200 yards long and 70 yards wide. Here was the place to catch the fish for my dinner.

Standing just clear of the white water I flicked the spoon into the run, pulling a few yards of line off the reel as I did so, and as I raised the rod to allow the line to run through the rings, the spoon was taken by a fish, near the bank and close to where I was standing. By great good luck the remaining portion of the slack line tightened on the drum of the reel and did not foul the butt of the rod or handle of the reel, as so often happens.

In a flash the fish was off down stream, the good reel singing a paean of joy as the line was stripped off it. The 50 yards of casting line followed a 100 yards of backing were gone, leaving in their passage burned furrows in the fingers of my left hand, when all at once, the mad rush ceased as abruptly as it had begun, and the line went dead.

The speculations one makes on these occasions chased each other through my mind, accompanied by a little strong language to ease my feelings. The hold had been good without question. The cast, made up a few days previously from short lengths of gut procured from the Pilot Gut Coy. had been carefully tied and tested. Suspicion centred on the split ring – possibly cracked on a stone on some previous occasion, it had now given way.

Sixty yards of the line are back on the reel, when the dead slack line is seen to curve to the left, and a moment later, is cutting a strong furrow up stream – the fish is still on, and is heading for the white water. Established here, pulling alternately from up stream, at right angles, and down stream fails to dislodge him. Time drags on and the conviction grows that the fish has gone, leaving the line hung up on a snag. Once again and just as hope is being abandoned the line goes slack, then tightens a moment later, as the fish goes madly down stream.

And now he appears to have made up his mind to leave this reach of river for the rapids below the pool. In one strong steady run he reaches the tail of the pool here, where the water fans out and shallows, he hesitates, and finally returns to the pool. A little later he shows on the surface for the first time and but for the fact that the taut line runs direct from the point of the rod to the indistinctly seen object on the far side of the pool, it would be impossible to believe that the owner of that great triangular fin, projecting five inches out of the water, had taken a fly spoon a yard or two from my feet.

Back in the depths of the pool, he is drawn inch by inch into slack water. To land a big fish single-handed on a trout rod, is not an easy accomplishment. Four times he was stranded with a portion of his great shoulders out of water and four times at my very cautious approach he lashed out, and returning to the pool, had to be fought back inch by inch. At the fifth attempt, with the butt of the rod held in the crook of my thumb and reversed, rings upward to avoid the handle of the reel coming into contact with him, he permits me to place one hand and then the other against his sides and very gently propel him through the shallow water up on to dry land.

A fish I had set out to catch, and a fish I had caught, but he would take no part in my dinner that night, for between me and camp lies three and a half miles of rough ground, half of which would have to be covered in the dark.

When sending away my camera I had retained the cotton cord I use for drawing the camera, which weighs eleven pounds, after me when I sit up in trees. One end of this cord was passed through the gills of the fish and out at his mouth, and securely tied in a loop. The other end was made fast to the branch of a tree. When the cord was paid out the fish lay snugly against a great slab of rock, in comparatively still water. Otter were the only danger and to scare them off, I made a flag of my handkerchief, and fixed the end of the improvised flag-staff in the bed of the river a little below the fish.

The sun was gilding the mountain tops next morning when I was back at the pool, and found the fish lying just where I had left it the previous evening. Unfastening the cord from the branch I wound it round my hand, as I descended the slab of rock towards the fish. Alarmed at my approach, or feeling the vibration of the cord, the fish suddenly galvanised into life and with a mighty splash dashed up stream. Caught at a disadvantage, I had no time to brace my feet on the sloping rock, before I was jerked headlong into the pool.

I have a great distaste for going over my depth in these submontane rivers, for the thought of being encircled by a hungry python is very repugnant to me, and I am glad there were no witnesses to the manner in which I floundered out of that pool. I had just scrambled out on the far side, with the fish still attached to my right hand, when the men, I had instructed to follow me from camp, arrived. Handing the fish over to them to take down to my camp on the bank of the river, I went on ahead to change and get my camera ready.

I had no means of weighing the fish and could only judge it by comparing its length with the height of the two men I had with me. It was nearly five feet long.

The weight of the fish is, however, immaterial for weights are soon forgotten, not so the surroundings in which the sport is indulged in. The steel blue of the fern-fringed pool where the water rests a little before cascading over rock and shingle to draw breath again in another pool, more beautiful than the one just left – the flash of the gaily-coloured king-fisher as he breaks the surface of the water, shedding a shower of diamonds from his wings as he rises with a chirp of delight, a silver minnow held firmly in his vermilion bill – the belling of the sambhar and the clear tuneful call of the cheetal apprising the jungle folk that the tiger, whose pug marks show wet on the sand where a few minutes before he crossed the river, is out in search of his dinner. These are the things that will not be forgotten and will live in my memory, the lodestone to draw me back to the beautiful valley, as yet unspoilt by the hand of man.

A LOST PARADISE

Forest Fires in the Hills

"Stop. You fools. Stop!"

The warning was not given a moment too soon.

I had kept an eye on the old Sal tree, since turning the corner in the wake of the men carrying my camp kit. Smoke was issuing from several boles in the hollow trunk, and only just in time I had noticed a tremor run through scorched leaves, the first indication that the supporting fibres were giving way. Slowly at first and then with a mighty rush and roar the proud giant of a hundred years strikes the road, hesitates and goes crashing down the khud side amid a smother of ashes and dislodged stones, to come to rest in the valley below.

Three days previously the forest had taken fire and for seventy-two hours a small band of foresters, assisted by all the available man-power of adjacent villages, had fought the flames. Not until the whole block of seventy-five square miles had been burnt out, had the devoted little band admitted defeat, and with swollen blood-shot eyes and blistered hands, turned their backs on the smouldering desolation.

The consensus of opinion was that the fire was incendiary. I was not inclined to agree with this opinion; for the serious loss of cattle and destruction of grazing grounds, resulting from the incendiary fires of 1922 was still green in the memory of the countryside and later, when camping in the area where the fire had originated, I came to the conclusion that smoke torches in the hands of careless honey collectors had been responsible for the conflagration.

It was late afternoon when I arrived at the edge of the burning forest. Earlier in the day a party of fire fighters, while sweeping a track along a subsidiary ridge preparatory to counter-firing, had seen a tiger coming towards them. In the ravine immediately below them a tiny stream had formed a miniature pool. When the tiger reached this pool the watching men saw she was carrying two small cubs.

Crossing to the far side of the water she laid the cubs on the wet ground under an overhanging rock, and turning – bounded back in the direction of the fire. Were the cubs she had rescued, one of which had a portion of its right hind leg burnt off, only a part of her young family and had the devoted mother gone back in the forlorn hope of saving the others? Only one of countless similar tragedies that were being enacted in the seventy-five square miles of forest and in the adjoining blocks, which were also on fire, for it was early May, the time of year when our foot-hills teem with young bird and animal life. The moment the tiger was safely out of sight, the fire party annexed the cubs, and when I arrived on the scene they were miles on their way to the Headquarters of the Range.

While camp was being made, a very simple operation when a 40 pound tent and camp bed are all that one needs, my old friend the Padhan (head-man) of the village I was camped near, paid me a visit and urged me to sit up over the pool, for, as he very rightly said, the tiger would be sure to return to look for her cubs. He was the same old friend, who twenty years previously had seen me miss a Kalij pheasant with my first barrel and after retrieving the bird from a long way down the khud, had remarked with disgust, that Europeans did not know how to shoot. "Flush a bird and then use two cartridges to kill it, was a waste of time and ammunition." When he, or any of his friends, wanted a pheasant or jungle-fowl they watched until the birds went to roost, and then when the birds were bunched together, one carefully aimed shot, and the whole covey came to earth as easily and simply as shaking ripe fruit from a mango tree. In twenty years his idea of sport had undergone no change, nor will it ever change.

My camp was only a short distance from the pool. Heat radiating from the smouldering forest made sleep impossible, and all through the long night I lay awake listening. No sound came up from the direction of the pool, and by morning I was convinced the tiger had passed to "The Happy Hunting Grounds". A very gallant lady, who a few months previously had held up a whole line of elephants, to give her mate time to get out of a beat.

Ten days earlier I had camped through this same forest, and it was then as near a wild paradise as it is possible to imagine. The air, perfumed with the scent from a million blossoms, throbbed with the mating call of all the songsters of the forest. In the valley, rutting cheetle stag brayed challenge to rutting stag, and karker called to karker, and now ten short days later, all is desolation! Ashes, where blossom and green verdure had been. Acrid smell of burnt mould and decaying flesh, where had been heavenly perfume, and a brooding silence, where once the air had pulsated with joyful song. A silence broken every now and again by the crash of a forest giant, as it comes to earth and goes skidding down the khud side, amid a smother of ashes and dislodged stones, to come to rest in the valley below.

A lost Paradise, in very truth!

PURNA GIRI AND ITS MYSTERIOUS LIGHTS

"There are more strange things in heaven and earth, Horatio, than are dreamt of in our philosophy."

Early in April of the present year, I was making a forced march into the hills, and at the end of a long day's walk, found myself, as night was drawing near, in a deep valley with a snow-fed river flowing along the bottom. For an hour I had been following the line of a long disused road which ran, some 100 feet above the river, along the precipitous south face of the sacred hill of Purna Giri.

When almost too dark to continue along the foot track, I came on a portion of the road that had been blasted out of the solid rock and had not suffered from the floods, which had carried away the rest of the road. On this ledge, some eight feet broad, I decided to make my camp for the night. The outer edge of the ledge was littered with stones fallen from above – none too safe a place in which to spend a night but it would have to serve, for a footwide track running across a hill in the form of a fever chart, was more than even a hill man could negotiate in the dark.

Camp was soon made, a simple matter when the ground is too hard for tent pegs and an "X" pattern bed is the sum total of one's camp furniture, and I was enjoying an after dinner smoke, when I noticed three lights on the hill across the river and about 150 yards away from me. April is the month for forest fires and it is quite a common sight to see dead wood burning days after a fire has swept through the forest. Half an hour, mayhap an hour later, one does not particularly notice the passage of time under the stars, two more lights appeared a little above the original three. Fanned by the strong wind blowing down the valley the smouldering embers in other dead wood had been brought to life and as I idly watched these new fires, the one on the left moved slowly down the hill and joined the middle one of the original three.

No fires these, but lights, all of a uniform size, about two feet in diameter and burning quite steadily without any flicker and without any trace of smoke. When shortly after, more lights appeared, some to the left and others further up the hill, an explanation presented itself. A potentate out on shikar had dropped a cartridge, or a hunting knife, and an army of men armed with lanterns was searching for the lost trifle. A strange explanation! Admitted, but many strange things happen in the independent territory on the far side of that snow-fed river.

My men were as interested in the lights as I was and as the river below us flowed without a ripple and the night was silent, in between the gusts of wind, I asked them if they could hear voices and received the answer that they could neither hear voices nor could they hear any sound from the fires. Further speculation was profitless and after a time the small camp settled down and was soon wrapped in slumber. Once during the night, some stones dislodged on the hill above us, came rattling down a side ravine, followed a second later by the alarm call of a ghooral; a leopard had spoilt his stalk by trusting his weight on a loose stone and showed his annoyance at the loss of a meal, by giving vent to his sawing call, echoed once and again from the wind-hollowed caves in the cliffs above.

A difficult march lay ahead, fifteen miles through forest and along the river bank and then a climb of 5,000 feet up the face of a steep hill to my objective, an oak, rhododendron, and bracken covered ridge 8,000 feet high. The men had been warned that a very early start would be made, and light was just beginning to show in the east when chota hazri was produced. Soon head and back loads were sorted and strapped and when all was ready for a start, I turned my attention to the hill across the river.

The sun was not far off rising and objects were now clearly visible. From crest to water's edge, and from water's edge to crest I scanned the hill, first with the naked eye and then with a powerful pair of field glasses, but not a sign of any human being could I see nor, reverting to my first theory, was there a burning log or stump in sight and it only needed a glance to see that the vegetation had not been burnt for a year. The hill was rock, from top to bottom, a few stunted trees growing where root hold had been obtained.

The place where the three first lights had appeared was sheer rock, partly overhanging, where a lizard might find a foothold, but where no human being, unless suspended by ropes from above, could possibly go. It still wanted a few minutes to sunrise and until the sun was two hours high no photograph could be taken. I had just decided that on my return journey I would make a point of arriving at this spot at midday, for the purpose of getting a photo, when my Brahmin bearer, who had been intently scanning the hill, spoke "The coolies have gone far sahib, and it were best not to linger alone at this place."

Nine days later, my mission in the hills accomplished, I camped in one of the most beautiful spots in the Himalayas. An emerald green plain, starting from dense sal forest, sloped gently down to the river and on this plain secure in their remoteness from carnivorous bipeds, cheetal and sambhar, either singly or in small groups were peacefully feeding – half a day's march down the valley, was the hill of lights.

My bearer, who had no luck with two of his children and was anxious to rear the third, begged leave to visit the sacred hill of Purna Giri. Accordingly next morning while I walked down the valley on photography intent, my bearer went up the hill to make offerings on his own behalf and a few enquiries on mine, for who should know more about the lights on the far side of the river, than the faquirs who attend the shrines on the sacred hill immediately above the hill of lights. By evening, both our missions were fulfilled. You have the result in the photographs before you. The result of my bearer's mission, time will reveal. For the rest, I give you the information he imparted to me that night, when comfortably tired after many days of strenuous walking, I smoked the after dinner pipe of peace.

Purna Giri dedicated to the worship of the Goddess Bhagbatti, the mother of increase, is accessible by two tracks, the one from the North-East being used by hillmen and the one from the South-West being used by the tens of thousands of pilgrims from the plains of India. These two tracks meet on the north face of the hill, a short distance from the summit. Near the junction is the first shrine, composed entirely of copper and large enough for a man to stand up in.

A rich mahajin from the plains of India promised the Goddess that if his request was granted, he would present her with a golden shrine. In due time the shrine arrived and was carried to the place where it now stands. Beyond this spot it was found impossible to move the shrine and on careful examination it was found that the shrine was made of copper overlaid with gold. Above the shrine and at the summit of the hill is the real shrine of Purna Giri, with a pinnacle of rock some fifty feet in height, which no one is permitted to climb, by the side of it.

Between the lower and upper shrines there is a difficult bit of ground, which children and the nervous negotiate in a basket slung on the back of a Hillman. Only those whom the Goddess permits are able to attain to the upper shrine; the others are struck blind and have to make their offerings at the lower shrine or, send them to the upper shrine, by hand of friends. These offerings consist of precious metals, sweets and cocoa-nuts.

Puja, at the upper shrine, starts at sunrise and ends at eleven o'clock; after this hour no one is allowed to pass the lower shrine.

In the days of long ago a faquir, more ambitious than his fellows, climbed the pinnacle of rock with the object of putting himself on an equality with the Goddess. Incensed at his disregard of orders, the Goddess hurled the faquir from the pinnacle of rock across the valley, to the hill on the far side of the snow-fed river. It is this faquir who, banished for ever from the sacred hill, worships the Goddess 2,000 feet above him, by lighting lamps for her. These lights only appear at certain times (I saw them on April 5) and are only visible to favoured people. The favour was accorded to me and the men with me, because we were on a mission to the hill folk, over whom the Goddess watches. It is unlikely that any pilgrims have seen the lights, for the shrines are situated on the North face of the hill and some little distance below the crest, on which no one is permitted to remain after 11 a.m. Further, the hill on which the lights appeared, is not visible from any point along the two tracks by which the shrines are approached.

I have told my tale and given you the explanation for the lights as it was given to me. You who are unable to accept that explanation can find your own, bearing the following points in mind: -

The lights did not appear simultaneously.
Were of a uniform size.
Were not affected by the wind.
Were able to move from one spot to another.

THE TERROR THAT WALKS BY NIGHT

An Episode of the Indian Jungle

However little faith we have in the superstitions we share with others – thirteen at a table – the passing of wine at dinner – walking under a ladder – etc. etc., our own private superstitions, though a source of amusement to our friends, are very real to us.

I do not know if sportsmen are more superstitious than the rest of mankind, but I do know that they take their superstitions very seriously. One of my friends invariably takes five cartridges, never more and never less, when he goes out after big game, and another as invariably takes seven cartridges. Another, who incidentally was the best known big game sportsman in Northern India, never started a winter shooting season without first killing a Mahseer. My own private superstition concerns snakes. When after man-eaters I have a deep-rooted conviction that however much I may try, all my efforts will be unavailing, until I have first killed a snake.

During the hottest days of one May I had from dawn to dark climbed innumerable miles up and down incredibly steep hills, and through thick thorn bushes that had left my hands and knees a mass of ugly scratches, in search of a very wary man-eater. I returned on that fifteenth evening, dog tired, to the little two-roomed forest bungalow I was staying at, to find a deputation of villagers waiting for me, with the very welcome news that the man-eater, a tiger, had been seen that day on the outskirts of their village. It was too late to do anything that night, so the deputation were provided with lanterns and sent home with strict injunctions that no one was to leave the village the following day.

The village was situated at the extreme end of the ridge on which the bungalow was, and because of its isolated position and the thick forest that surrounded it, had suffered more from the depredations of the tiger than any other village in the district. The victims from this village were two women and one man.

I had made one complete circle of the village the following morning and had done the greater part of a second circle, when after negotiating a difficult scree of shale I came on a little "nala" made by the rush of rain water down the steep hill-side. A glance up and down this nala satisfied me that the tiger was not in it, and then a movement just in front of me, and about twenty-five feet away caught my eye and it was not until the head had been raised some two or three feet from the ground and the hood expanded that I realised it was a Hamadryad. It was the most beautiful snake I had ever seen. The throat, as I faced it was deep orange-red shading to golden-yellow where the body met the ground. The back, olive green, was banded by ivory coloured chevrons, and some four feet of its length from the tail upwards was polished black, with white chevrons. In length the snake was between thirteen and fourteen feet. One hears many tales about Hamadryads, their aggressiveness when disturbed, and the speed at which they can travel. If as it seemed about to do, the snake attacked, up or down hill, I would be at a disadvantage, but if across the shale scree, I felt that I could hold my own. A shot at the expanded hood, the size of a small plate, would have ended the tension, but the rifle in my hands was a heavy one and I had no intention of disturbing the tiger that had shown up after so many days of weary waiting and toil. After an interminably long minute, during which time the only movement was the flicking in and out of a long and quivering forked tongue, the snake closed his hood, lowered his head to the ground and turning, made off up the opposite slope. Without taking my eyes off the reptile I groped with my hand on the hillside and picked up a stone that filled my hand as comfortably as a cricket ball. The snake had just reached a sharp ridge of hard clay when the stone, launched with the utmost energy I was capable of, struck it on the back of the head. The blow would have killed any other snake outright, but the only and very alarming effect it had on the Hamadryad was to make it whip round and come straight back towards me. A second and a larger stone fortunately caught it on the neck when it had covered half the distance between us and after that the rest was easy. With a great feeling of satisfaction I completed the second circle round the village, and though it proved as fruitless as the first, I was elated at having killed a snake for now for the first time in many days I had a feeling that my search for the man-eater would be successful.

The following day I again searched the forest surrounding the village and towards evening found the fresh pug-marks of the tiger under a bush at the edge of a field over-looking the village. The occupants of the village, numbering about a hundred, were by now thoroughly alarmed, and leaving them with the assurance that I would return early next day I set out on my lonely four-mile walk back to the forest bungalow.

To walk with safety, through forests or along deserted roads in an area in which a man-eating tiger is operating, calls for the utmost caution and the strict observance of many rules. It is only when the hunter has repeatedly been the hunted that the senses can be attuned to the required pitch, and those rules be strictly adhered to, the breaking of which would provide the man-eater with an easy victim.

My reader may ask "Why a lonely walk" when I probably had men with me in camp? The question would be a very natural one and for the sake of brevity I will give as short an answer as possible. First then, because one is apt to get careless and rely too much on one's companions. Second, because in a mix-up with a tiger one has a better chance when one is alone; and third, because risks in sport should not be shared.

The next morning as I approached the village I saw an eager throng of men awaiting me, and when within ear-shot, I was greeted with the gratifying news that a buffalo had been killed during the night. The animal had been killed in the village and after being dragged some distance along the ridge had been taken down into a narrow, deep, and very heavily wooded valley on the north side of the hill.

A careful reconnaissance from a projecting rock on the ridge satisfied me that an approach down the steep hill, along the line of the drag, would not be advisable and that the only thing to do was to make a wide detour, enter the valley from the lower end and work up to the spot where I expected to find the kill.

This manoeuvre was successfully accomplished and by mid-day I arrived at the spot marked from above where the valley flattened out for a hundred yards, before going straight up three hundred yards to the ridge above. It was at the upper end of this bit of ground that I expected to find the kill, and with luck, the tiger. The long and difficult climb up the valley through dense thickets of thorn bush and stunted bamboo had brought out a bath of sweat, and as it was not advisable to take on a job where quick firing might be necessary, with sweaty hands, I sat down for a much needed rest and a smoke.

The ground in front of me was strewn with large smooth boulders among which a tiny stream meandered, forming wherever possible small crystal-clear pools. Shod with the thinnest of rubber-soled shoes, the going over these boulders was ideal for my purpose and when I had cooled and dried I set off to stalk the kill in the hope of finding the tiger lying asleep near it. When three-quarters of the ground had been covered I caught sight of the kill tucked away under a thick bank of ferns, and about twenty-five yards from where the hill went steeply up the ridge. The tiger was not in sight and very cautiously drawing level with the kill I took up my position on a flat boulder to scan every inch of ground visible to me.

The premonition of impending danger is too well known and established a fact to need any comment. For three or four minutes, may have been longer, I had stood perfectly still with no thought of danger and then all at once I became aware that the tiger was looking at me at a very short range. The same sense that had conveyed this feeling of impending danger to me had evidently operated in the same way on the tiger and awakened him from his sleep. To my left front were some thick bushes, growing on a bit of flat ground. On these bushes, distant fifteen to twenty feet from me, and about the same distance from the kill my interest centred. Presently the bushes were gently stirred and the next second I caught sight of the tiger going full speed up the steep hill-side. Before I could get the rifle to bear on him he disappeared behind a creeper-covered tree and it was not until he had covered sixty or seventy yards that I again saw him, as he was springing up the face of a rock. At my shot, fired as he was springing, he fell backwards and came tearing down the hill, bringing an avalanche of stones with him. A broken back I concluded and just as I was wondering how best to deal with him when he should arrive all-of-a-heap at my feet, the roaring ceased and the next minute, as much to my relief as to my disappointment, I saw him going full-out, and apparently unwounded, across the side of the hill. The momentary glances I caught of him offered no shot worth taking, and with a crash through some dry bamboos he disappeared round the shoulder of the hill into the next valley. My bullet I subsequently found, fired at an angle of seventy-five degrees, had hit the tiger on the left elbow and chipped out a big section from that bone, which has by some cynical humourist been named the "funny bone". Carrying on, the bullet had struck the rock and splashing back had delivered a smashing blow on the point of the jaw. Neither wound, however painful it may have been, was fatal, and the only result of my following up the very light blood trail into the next valley was to be growled at from a dense thorn thicket, to enter which would have been suicidal.

My shot had been heard in the village and an expectant crowd were waiting for me on the ridge and were even more disappointed, if that were possible, than I was at the failure of my carefully planned and as carefully executed stalk.

On visiting the kill the following morning I was very pleased and not a little surprised to find that the tiger had returned to it during the night and taken a light meal. The only way now of getting a second shot was to sit up over the kill and here a difficulty presented itself. There were no suitable trees within convenient distance of the kill, and the very unpleasant experience I had had on a former occasion, had effectively cured me of sitting at night on the ground for a man-eater. While still undecided where to sit I heard the tiger call some distance down the valley, up which I had climbed the previous day. The calling of the tiger offered me a very welcome chance of shooting it in the most pleasant way it is possible of bringing one of these animals to bag. The conditions under which a tiger can be called up are (a) when rampaging through the forest looking for a mate, and (b) when lightly wounded. It goes without saying that the sportsman must be able to call sufficiently well to deceive the tiger, and that the call must come from a spot to which the tiger will quite naturally come – a dense thicket, or a patch of heavy grass – and that he must be prepared to take his shot at a very close range. I am quite certain that many sportsmen will be skeptical of the statement that I have made that a lightly wounded tiger will come to a call. I would ask all such to reserve their judgment, until they have tried the experiment for themselves. On this particular occasion, however, though the tiger answered me, call for call, for upwards of an hour, he refused to come any nearer, and I attributed my failure to the fact that I was calling from the spot where the previous day he had met with an unfortunate experience.

The tree I finally selected was growing on the very edge of a perpendicular bank and had a convenient branch about eight feet from the ground. When sitting on this branch I would be thirty feet from, and directly above, the boulder-strewn ravine up which I expected the tiger to come. The question of the tree settled, I returned to the ridge where I had instructed my men to meet me with breakfast.

By four o'clock in the evening I was comfortably seated on the branch and prepared for a long and hard sit-up. Before leaving my men I had instructed them to "coo-ee" to me from the ridge at sun-rise next morning and if I answered with the call of a leopard to sit tight, but if they received no answer, to form two parties with as many villagers as they could collect and come down either side of the valley, shouting and throwing stones.

I have acquired the habit of sleeping in any position on a tree and as I was tired, the evening did not pass unpleasantly, and as the setting sun was gilding the hill-tops above me, I was roused to full consciousness by the alarm call of a langoor, (Entellus monkey). I soon located the monkey sitting in a tree-top on the far side of the valley and as it was looking in my direction I concluded it had mistaken me for a leopard. The alarm call was repeated at short intervals, and finally ceased as darkness came on. Hour after hour I strained my eyes and ears and was suddenly startled by a stone, rolling down the hill side, and striking my tree. The stone was followed by the stealthy padding of a heavy soft-footed animal, unmistakably the tiger. At first I comforted myself with the thought that his coming in this direction instead of up the valley was accidental, but this thought was soon dispelled, when he started to emit low deep growls from immediately behind me. Quite evidently he had come into the valley while I was on the ridge having breakfast, and taking up a position on the hill, where the monkey had later seen him, had watched me climbing into the tree. Here was a situation I had not counted on and one that needed careful handling. The branch that provided a comfortable seat while day-light lasted, admitted of no change of position in the dark. I could have of course fired off my rifle into the air but the terrible results I have seen following an attempt to drive away a tiger at very close quarters by discharging a gun, dissuaded me from taking this action. Further, even if the tiger had not attacked, the discharge of the heavy rifle so near him would probably have made him leave the locality and all my toil would have gone for nothing. I knew the tiger would not spring, for that would have carried him straight down a drop of thirty feet on to the rocks below, but there was no need for him to spring, for by standing on his hind legs he could easily reach me. Lifting the rifle off my lap and reversing it, I pushed the barrel between my left arm and side, depressing the muzzle and slipping up the safety catch as I did so. This movement was greeted with a deeper growl than any that had preceded it. If the tiger now reached up for me he would in all probability come in contact with the rifle, round the trigger of which my fingers were crooked, and even if I failed to kill him the confusion following on my shot would give me a sporting chance of climbing higher up into the tree. Time dragged by on leaden feet, and eventually tiring of prowling about the hill-side and growling, the tiger sprang across a little ravine on my left and a few minutes later I heard the welcome sound of a bone being cracked at the kill. At last I was able to relax in my uncomfortable position and the only sounds I heard for the rest of the night came from the direction of the kill.

The sun had been up but a few minutes and the valley was still in deep shadow when my men "coo-eed" from the ridge and almost immediately afterwards I caught sight of the tiger making off at a fast canter up, and across, the hill on my left. In the uncertain light and with my night-long strained eyes the shot was a very difficult one, but I took it, and had the satisfaction of seeing the bullet going home. Turning with a great roar, he came straight for my tree, and as he was in the act of springing, the second bullet, with great good fortune, crashed into his chest. Diverted in his spring by the impact of the heavy bullet, he struck the tree just short of me, and ricocheting off it went headlong into the valley below, where his fall was broken by one of the small pools already alluded to. Floundering out of the water which he left dyed red with his blood, he went lumbering down the valley and out of sight. Fifteen hours on the hard branch had cramped every muscle in my body, and it was not until I had swarmed down the tree, staining my clothes in the great gouts of blood the tiger had left on it, and had massaged my stiff limbs, that I was able to follow him. He had gone but a short distance and I found him lying dead at the foot of a rock in another pool of water. Contrary to my orders, the men collected on the ridge on hearing my shot, and the tiger's roar, followed by a second shot, came helter skelter down the hill. Arrived at the blood-stained tree, at the foot of which my soft hat was lying, they not unnaturally concluded I had been carried off by the tiger. Hearing their shouts of alarm I called out to them, and again they came running down the valley, only to be brought up with a gasp of dismay when they saw my blood stained clothes. Reassured on this point, a moment later they were crowding around the tiger. A stout sapling was soon cut and lashed to it by creepers, the tiger, with no little difficulty, and a great deal of shouting, was carried to the village.

The accompanying photograph is of the tiger and the father of one of its last victims, an only son, who two days before his untimely death had, to the great joy of his father, been accepted as a recruit in that famous Regiment, The 2nd Battalion Garhwal Rifles.

WILD LIFE IN THE VILLAGE: AN APPEAL

Published in the "Review of the Week", 31-8-1932

It was a small village of some 16 ploughs differing in no respect from hundreds of similar villages, scattered throughout the length of the Bhabar. Originally the village had been surrounded by tree jungle intercepted with grass and in this virgin jungle lived all the numerous denizens of the wild. To protect their crops the villagers erected thorn fences round their fields. As an additional safeguard a member of the depressed class was encouraged to settle in the village whose duty it was to watch the crops at night and see they were not damaged by stray cattle or wild animals.

Owing to the abundance of game, tigers did not interfere with the village cattle and I cannot remember a single case of cow or bullock having been killed by a tiger. In the course of time, a great change took place, not only in the villagers themselves, but also in the jungle surrounding the village. Hindus who formerly looked upon the taking of life as against their religious principles, were now clamouring for gun licences and were competing with each other in the indiscriminate slaughter of game. As profits from the sale of game increased, field work was neglected and land began to go out of cultivation. Simultaneously lantana, introduced into Haldwani as a pot plant, started to kill out the grass and basonta, until the village was surrounded with a dense growth of this noxious weed. Government now stepped in, and at great expense, built a pucca wall all round the village. The building of this wall freed the villagers from the necessity of erecting fences and watching their crops, and gave them more time to devote to the killing of the game. This heavy and unrestricted shooting of deer had the inevitable consequence of disturbing the balance in nature with the result that tigers and leopards, that had hitherto lived on game, were now forced to live on the village cattle.

One morning in May of the present year I arrived in the village and pitched my tent in a little clearing just outside the cultivated land. News of my arrival soon spread through the village and in a short time a dozen men were squatting in front of my tent. One and all had the same tale to tell. A tiger had taken up its quarters in the lantana, and in the course of two years had killed 150 head of cattle, and unless it was destroyed the village would have to be abandoned.

While the men were pouring out their tale of woe, I observed a pair of vultures circling low over a narrow stretch of lantana, running between the village wall and the public road. The two vultures were soon joined by others; so picking up a rifle I set off to investigate. Progress through the lantana was difficult but with the aid of a good hunting knife a way was eventually cut, and the remains of a horse, killed the previous day found. There were plenty of pug marks round the kill, little of which remained, and it was easy to locate the tiger from his low continuous growling, but impossible to see him in the dense cover. Returning to the road, which was only 40 yards from the kill, and little used at this time of year, I concealed myself behind a bush in the hope that the tiger would follow me to see if I had left the locality, quite a natural thing for it to do. Half an hour later the tiger walked out on to the road and gave me an easy shot, as he stood facing me.

That evening after I had skinned the tiger – he was a very old animal and I took four old bullets and nine pellets of buckshot out of him – I called the villagers together, and made an appeal to them on behalf of the few remaining deer in the jungle. On the opposite side of the village from my camp, irrigation water had been allowed to flow into the jungle. Over this water machans had been built in the trees, and in these machans men sat through the heat of the day, and all night long on moon-light nights, and shot down animals that came to drink. There was no other water within miles and if a thirst-maddened animal avoided one machan, it fell victim to the next. I told the villagers that God had given water free for all, and that it was a shameful thing for man to sit over the water God had provided and shoot His creatures when they came to drink. To do this was to lower themselves below the level of a corpse-eating hyaena, for even he, the lowest of all creation, did not lie in wait to kill defenceless animals while they were drinking. The men listened to me in silence, and when I had done, said they had not looked at the matter in this light, and they promised that they would take down the machans they had erected, and in future would not molest the animals that came to the vicinity of the village to drink.

I stayed in the locality several weeks, taking bird and animal pictures, and am glad to say the men kept their promise. I believe that much of the slaughter of deer that is daily taking place throughout the length and breadth of the Bhabar and Tarai, would cease if an appeal was made to the better feelings of men.

I do not exaggerate the damage that is being done to our fauna by shooting over water. Let me give you but one instance. An acquaintance of mine living in a village in the Bhabar adjoining me, in one hot season, over one small pool of water shot, with a single barrel muzzle-loading gun, 60 head of cheetal and sambhar, which he sold in a near-by bazar at the rate of Rs 5 per cheetal and Rs 10 per sambhar. It is no exaggeration to say that the banks of every little stream and every pool of water in the vicinity of Bhabar villages, are soaked with the blood of animals that never took toll of a single blade of the villagers' crops. I assert without fear of contradiction, that for every shot fired on cultivated land from guns provided for crop protection, a hundred shots are fired in the jungle over water. Pigs and neelgai are the only wild animals that damage the crops in the Bhabar to any extent, and to keep them out of cultivated land Government has expended lakhs of rupees in building pucca walls.

It is asserted that in recent years tigers have increased. With this assertion I do not agree. It is a fact that more cattle are being killed every year, this is not due to the tigers having increased, but due to the balance in nature having been disturbed by the unrestricted slaughter of game and also to some extent to tigers having been driven out of their natural haunts, where they were seldom or never seen by man, by the activities of the Forest Department.

A country's fauna is a sacred trust, and I appeal to you not to betray this trust. Shooting over water, shooting over salt-licks, natural and artificial, shooting birds in the close season and when roosting at night, encouraging permit-holders to shoot hinds, fencing off of large areas of forest, and the extermination by the Forest Department of all game within these areas, making of unnecessary motor tracks through the forest and shooting from motor cars, absence of sanctuaries, and the burning of forests by the Forest Department and by villagers, at a time when forests are full of young life, are all combining to one end – the extermination of our fauna. If we do not bestir ourselves now, it will be to our discredit that the fauna of our province was exterminated in our generation and under our very eyes, while we looked on and never raised a finger to prevent it.

THE CHOWGARH TIGERS

The map of Eastern Kumaon that hangs on the wall before me is marked with a number of crosses, and below each cross is a date; the former indicate the locality, and the latter the date of the officially recorded human victims of the man-eating tiger of Chowgarh. There are sixty-four crosses on the map. I do not claim that this is a correct tally, for the map was posted up by me for two years and during this period all kills were not reported to me; further, victims who were only mauled and who died subsequently, have not been awarded a cross and a date.

The first cross is dated 15-12-1925 and the last 11-4-30. The distance between the extreme crosses, North to South, is 50 miles, and East to West 30 miles, an area of 1500 square miles of mountains where the snow lies deep in the winter, and the valleys are scorchingly hot in summer. Over this area the Chowgarh tiger had established a reign of terror. Villages of varying size, some with a population of a hundred or more, and others with only a small family or two, are scattered throughout the area. Foot paths, beaten hard by bare feet, connect the villages. Some of these paths pass through thick forest, and when a man-eater has rendered their passage dangerous, inter village communication is carried on by shouting. Standing on a commanding point, maybe a big rock, or the roof of a house, a man "Cooees" to attract the attention of the people in a neighbouring village; and when the cooee is answered, the message is shouted across in a high pitched voice. From village to village the message is tossed and is broadcast throughout large areas in an incredibly short space of time.

It was at a district conference in February 1929 that I found myself committed to have a try for this tiger. There were at that time three man-eaters in the Kumaon Division, and as the Chowgarh tiger had done most damage, I promised to go in pursuit of it first.

The map with the crosses and dates furnished to me by Government, showed that the man-eater was most active in the villages on the North and East face of the Kala Agar ridge. This ridge, some forty miles in length, rises to a height of 8500 feet, and is thickly wooded along the crest. A Forest road runs along the north face of the ridge, in some places passing for miles through dense forests of oak and rhododendron, and in other places forming a boundary between the forest and cultivated land. In one place the road forms a loop, and in this loop is situated the Kala Agar Forest bungalow. This bungalow was my objective, and after a four days' march, culminating in a stiff climb of 4000 feet, I arrived at it one evening in April 1929. The last human victim in the area was a young man of twenty-two, who had been killed while out grazing cattle, and while I was having breakfast the morning after my arrival, the grandmother of the young man came to see me.

She informed me that the man-eater had, without any provocation, killed the only relative she had in the world. After giving me her grandson's history from the day he was born, and extolling his virtues, she pressed me to accept her three milch buffaloes, to use as bait for the tiger, saying that if I kill the tiger with the help of her buffaloes, she would have the satisfaction of feeling that she had assisted in avenging her grandson. These full-grown buffaloes were of no use to me, but knowing that refusal to accept them would give offence, I thanked the old lady, and assured her I would draw on her for bait, as soon as I had used up the four young male buffaloes I had brought with me. The head men of nearby villages had now assembled, and from them I learned that the tiger had last been seen ten days previously at a village twenty miles away, on the Eastern slope of the ridge, where it had killed and eaten a man and his wife.

A trail ten days old was not worth following up, and after a long discussion with the Headmen, I decided to make for Dalkania village on the Eastern slope of the ridge. This village is about ten miles from Kala Agar Forest Bungalow and about five miles from the village where the man and his wife had been killed.

From the number of crosses, Dalkania and the villages adjoining it, had earned, it appeared that the tiger had its headquarters in the vicinity of these villages.

After breakfast next morning I left Kala Agar following the Forest Road, which I was informed would take me to the end of the ridge, where I would have to leave the road and take a path two miles down hill to Dalkania. This road running right to the end of the ridge through dense forest was very little used, and examining it for tracks as I went along, I arrived at the point where the path took off, at about 2 p.m. Here I met a number of men from Dalkania. They had heard of my intention of camping at their village and had come up to the ridge to inform me that the tiger had that morning attacked a party of women, while cutting their crops in a village ten miles to the North.

The men carrying my camp equipment had done eight miles and were quite willing to carry on, but on learning from the villagers that the path to this village, ten miles away, was very rough and ran through dense forest, I decided to send my men with the villagers to Dalkania, and visit the scene of the tiger's attack alone. My servant immediately set about preparing a substantial meal and at 3 p.m., having fortified myself, I set out on my ten miles walk. Ten miles under favourable conditions is a comfortable two and half hours' walk, but here, the conditions were anything but favourable. The track running along the East face of this hill wound in and out through deep ravines and was bordered alternately by rocks, dense undergrowth and trees; and when every obstruction capable of concealing sudden death, in the form of a hungry man-eater, had to be approached with caution, progress was of necessity slow. I was still several miles from my objective, when the declining day warned me it was time to call a halt.

In any other area, sleeping under the stars on a bed of dry leaves would have ensured a restful night, but here, to sleep on the ground would have been to court death in a very unpleasant form. Long practice in selecting a suitable tree, and the ability to dispose myself comfortably in it, has made sleeping up aloft a simple matter. On this occasion I selected an oak tree, and with the rifle tied securely to a branch, had been asleep for some hours, when I was awakened by the rustling of several animals under the tree. The sound moved on and presently I heard the scraping of claws on bark and realised that a family of bears were climbing some karphal trees I had noticed growing a little way down the hill side. Bears are very quarrelsome when feeding, and sleep was impossible until they had eaten their fill and moved on.

The sun had been up a couple of hours when I arrived at the village, which consisted of two huts and a cattle shed, in a clearing of five acres, surrounded by forest. The small community were in a state of terror and were overjoyed to see me. The wheat field, a few yards from the huts, where the tiger, with belly to ground, had been detected only just in time, stalking the three women cutting the crop, was eagerly pointed out to me. The man who had first seen the tiger and given the alarm told me the tiger had retreated into the jungle, where it had been joined by a second tiger, and that together the two tigers had gone down the hill-side into the valley below. The occupants of the two huts had had no sleep, for the tigers, baulked of their prey, had called at short intervals throughout the night, and had only ceased calling a little before my arrival. This statement, that there were two tigers, confirmed the reports I had already received, that the man-eater was accompanied by a full grown cub.

Our hill folk are very hospitable, and when the villagers learned that my camp was at Dalkania, they offered to prepare a meal for me. This I knew would strain the resources of the small community, so I asked for a dish of tea, but as there was no tea in the village, I was given a very liberal drink of fresh milk, sweetened to excess with jaggree, a very sustaining, and not unpleasant drink – when one gets used to it. At the request of my hosts, I mounted guard, while the remaining portion of the wheat crop was cut; and at mid-day, taking the good wishes of the people with me, I went down into the valley, in the direction in which the tigers had been heard calling.

The valley, starting from the water-shed of three rivers, Ladhya, Nandhour and Eastern Goula, runs South West, and is densely wooded at its upper end where I entered it. Tracking was impossible, and my only hope of seeing the tigers was to attract them, or helped by the calling of sambhar, karkar, or birds, to stalk them.

To those who may be inclined to indulge in the sport of man-eater hunting on foot, it will be of interest to know that the animals and birds of the jungle, and the four winds of Heaven alone make this sport possible. In this article space will not permit of my giving the names of the animals and birds on whose alarm-calls the sportsman depends for his safety and knowledge of his quarry's movements for in a country in which a walk up or down hill of a couple of miles might mean a difference in altitude of as many thousand feet, it will be realised that the variety of fauna is considerable. The wind however, at all altitudes, remains a constant factor and a few words relevant to its importance in connection with man-eaters will not be out of place.

Tigers do not know that human beings have no sense of scent, and when a tiger becomes a man-eater, it treats human beings exactly as it treats sambhar and other wild animals, that is, it approaches its intended victims up wind, or lies in wait on the lee side of where it expects its victim to pass. The significance of this will be apparent, when it is realised that while the sportsman is trying to get a sight of the tiger, the tiger, in all probability is trying to stalk the sportsman, or is lying up in wait for him. The contest, owing to the tiger's height, colouring and ability to move without making a sound, would be very unequal were it not for the wind factor operating in favour of the sportsman. In all cases where killing is done by stealth, the victim is approached from behind. This being so, it would be impossible for the sportsman to enter dense jungle, in which he has every reason to believe a man-eater is lurking, unless he was capable of making full use of the currents of air. For example, assuming that the sportsman has to proceed, owing to the nature of the ground, in the direction from which the wind is blowing, the danger would lie behind him, where he would be least able to deal with it, but by frequently tacking across the wind he could keep the danger alternately to right and left of him. In print this scheme may not appear very attractive, but in practice it works; and short of walking backwards, I do not know of a better method of going upwind through dense jungle with any reasonable measure of safety.

By evening I had reached the upper end of the valley, without having seen the tigers, and without having received any indication of their presence in the jungle. The only habitation then in sight was a cattle shed high up on the North side of the valley.

I was careful in the selection of a tree on this second night and was rewarded by an undisturbed night's rest. Not long after dark the tigers called, and a few minutes later two shots from a muzzle loader came echoing down the valley, followed by a lot of shouting from the graziers at the cattle station.

Thereafter the night was silent. By the afternoon of the following day I had explored every bit of the valley and was making my way up a grassy slope intent on rejoining my camp at Dalkania, when I heard a long drawn out "cooee" from the direction of the cattle shed. The "cooee" was repeated once again, and on my sending back an answering call, I saw a man climb on a projecting rock, and from this vantage point he shouted across the valley, to ask if I was the sahib who had come from Naini Tal to shoot the man-eater. On my telling him I was, he informed me that his cattle had stampeded out of a ravine on my side of the valley at about mid-day, and that on counting them on arrival at the cattle station he found one – a white cow – was missing.

He suspected the cow had been killed by the tiger he had heard calling the previous night, in a ravine half a mile to the West of where I was standing. Thanking him for this information I set off to investigate the ravine. I had gone but a short distance along the edge of the ravine, when I came on the tracks of the stampeding cattle and following these tracks back, I had no difficulty in finding the spot where the cow had been killed. After killing the cow, the tiger had dragged it down a steep hill side into the ravine. An approach along the drag was not advisable, so going down into the valley I made a wide detour and approached the spot where I expected the kill to be, from the other side of the ravine. This side of the ravine was less steep than the side down which the kill had been dragged, and was deep in young bracken – ideal ground for stalking over. Step by step I made my way through the bracken, which reached above my waist and when some thirty yards from the bed of the ravine, a movement in front of me caught my eye. A white leg was suddenly thrust up into the air and violently agitated, and next moment there was a deep throated growl – the tigers were on the kill and were having a difference of opinion over some toothsome morsel. For several minutes, I stood perfectly still; the leg continued to be agitated, but the growl was not repeated. A nearer approach was not advisable, for even if I succeeded in covering the thirty yards without being seen, and managed to kill one of the tigers, the other, as likely as not, would blunder into me, and the ground I was on would give me no chance of defending myself. Twenty yards to my left and about the same distance from the tigers, there was an out-crop of rock, some 10 to 15 feet in height. If I could reach this rock without being seen, I would, in all probability, get an easy shot at the tigers. Dropping on hands and knees and pushing the rifle before me, I crawled through the bracken to the shelter of the rock, paused a minute to regain my breath, and then climbed the rock. When my eyes were level with the top, I saw the two tigers. One was eating at the hind quarters of the cow, while the other was near by licking its paws. Both tigers appeared to be about the same size, but the one that was licking its paws was several shades lighter than the other; and concluding that she was the old man-eater, I aligned the sights on her, and fired. At my shot she reared up and fell backwards, while the other bounded down the ravine and was out of sight before I could press the second trigger. The tiger I had shot did not move again, and after pelting it with stones to make sure it was dead, I approached and met with a great disappointment; for at a glance at close quarters shewed me that I had made a mistake and shot the cub – a mistake that during the ensuing twelve months cost the district fifteen lives and incidentally nearly cost me my own life.

Disappointment was to a certain extent mitigated by the thought that this young tigress, even if she had not actually killed any human beings herself, had probably assisted the old tigress to kill, and in any case, having been nurtured on human flesh, she could without question be classed as a potential man-eater.

Skinning a tiger single-handed with the requisite appliances is an easy job, but here the task was anything but easy, for the only appliance I had was a small penknife; and although there was no actual danger to be apprehended from the man-eater, for tigers never kill in excess of their requirements, there was the uneasy feeling in the back of my mind, that the tigress had returned and was watching my every movement.

The sun was near setting before the arduous task was completed, and as I would have to spend another night in the jungles I decided to remain where I was. The tigress was a very old animal, as I could see from the pug marks, and having lived all her life in a district in which there are nearly as many firearms as men to use them, had nothing to learn about men and their ways. Even so, there was just a chance that she might return to the kill some time during the night, and remain in the vicinity until light came in the morning.

My selection of a tree was of necessity limited, and the one I spent that night in proved, by morning, to be the most uncomfortable tree I had ever spent twelve hours in. The tigress called at intervals throughout the night, and as morning drew near the calling became fainter and fainter, and eventually died away on the ridge above me.

Cramped, and stiff, and with my clothes clinging to me, for it had rained for an hour during the night, I descended the tree when objects were clearly visible and tying the tiger's skin up in my coat, I set off for Dalkania.

I have never weighed a tiger's skin when green, and if the skin, plus the head and paws which I carried for fifteen miles that day weighed 40 lbs at the start, I would have taken my oath it weighed 200 lbs before I reached my destination.

In the courtyard, flagged with great slabs of blue slate, and common to a dozen houses, I found my men in conference with a hundred or more villagers. My approach, along a yard wide lane, between the houses, had not been observed and the welcome I received when, bedraggled and covered with blood I staggered into the circle of squatting men, will live in my memory as long as memory lasts.

My 40 lb tent had been pitched in a field of stubble a hundred yards from the village, and I had hardly reached it before tea was laid out for me on a table improvised out of a couple of suitcases, and planks borrowed from the village. I was told later by the villagers, that my men, who had been with me for years and had accompanied me on several similar expeditions, refusing to believe the man-eater had claimed another victim, had kept a kettle on the boil night and day, in anticipation of my return.

A hot bath, taken of necessity in the open and an ample dinner followed hard on the pot of tea; and I was thinking of turning in for the night when a flash of lightning succeeded by a loud peal of thunder heralded the approach of a storm. Tent pegs are of little use in a field, so long stakes were hurriedly procured and securely driven into the ground, and to these stakes the tent ropes were tied. For further safety all the available ropes in camp were criss-crossed over the tent and lashed to the stakes. The storm only lasted an hour and was one of the worst the little tent had ever weathered. Several of the guy ropes were torn from the canvas, but the stakes and criss-cross ropes held. Most of my things were soaked through and a little stream, several inches deep was running from end to end of the tent; my bed, however, was comparatively dry, and by 10 o'clock my men were safely lodged behind locked doors in the house the villagers had placed at their disposal, while I, with a loaded rifle for company, settled down for a sleep which lasted for twelve hours.

The following day was occupied in drying my kit and in cleaning and pegging out the tiger's skin. While these operations were in progress the villagers, who had taken a holiday from their field work, crowded round to hear my experiences and to tell me theirs. Every man present had lost a relative, and several bore tooth and claw marks, inflicted by the man-eater, which they would carry to their graves. My regret at having lost an opportunity was not endorsed by the assembled men. True, there had originally been only one man-eater; but of recent months, rescue parties who had gone out to recover the remains of human victims, had found two tigers on the kills, and only a fortnight previously a man and his wife had been killed simultaneously, which was proof sufficient for them that both tigers were established man-eaters.

My tent was on a spur of the hill, and commanded an extensive view. Immediately below me was the valley of the

Nandhar river, with a hill, devoid of any cultivation, rising to a height of 9000 feet on the far side. As I sat on the edge of the terraced fields that evening with a pair of binoculars in my hand and the Government map spread out beside me, the villagers pointed out the exact position where twenty human beings had been killed during the past three years. These kills were more or less evenly distributed over an area of forty square miles.

The forests in this area were open to grazing and on the cattle paths leading to them I decided to tie up my four young buffaloes.

During the following ten days no news was received of the tigress and I spent the time visiting the buffaloes in the morning, searching the forests in the day, and tying up the buffaloes in the evening. On the eleventh day my hopes were raised by a report that a cow had been killed in a ravine on the hill above my tent. A visit to the kill, however satisfied me that the cow had been killed by an old leopard whose pug marks I had repeatedly seen. The villagers complained that the leopard had for several years been taking toll of their cattle and goats, so I decided to sit up for it. A cave close to the dead cow gave me the cover I needed. I had not been long in the cave when I caught sight of the leopard coming down the opposite side of the ravine, and was raising my rifle for a shot, when I heard a very agitated voice from the direction of the village calling to me.

There could be but one reason for this urgent call, and grabbing up my hat I dashed out of the cave, much to the consternation of the leopard, who first flattened himself out on the ground, and then with an angry woof went bounding back the way he had come, while I scrambled up my side of the ravine; and arriving at the top, shouted to the man that I was coming and set off at top speed to join him.

The man had run up the hill all the way from the village, and when he regained his breath he informed me that a woman had just been killed by the man-eater, about half a mile on the far side of the village. As we ran down the hill-side I saw a crowd of people collected in the courtyard already alluded to. Once again my approach through the narrow lane was not observed, and looking over the heads of the assembled men, I saw a girl sitting on the ground.

The upper part of her clothing had been torn off her young body, and with head thrown back and hands resting on the ground behind to support her, she sat without sound or movement, other than the heaving up and down of her breast, in the hollow which the blood, that was flowing down her face and neck, was collecting in a sticky, congealed mass. My presence was soon detected and a way made for me to approach the girl. While I examined her wounds, a score of people all talking together, informed me that the attack on the girl had been made on comparatively open ground, in full view of a number of people, including the girl's husband – that alarmed at their combined shouts the tiger had left the girl and retreated in the direction of the forest – that leaving the girl for dead, where she had fallen, they had run back to the village to inform me that subsequently the girl had regained consciousness and returned to the village – that she would, without doubt die of her injuries in a few minutes and that they would then carry her back to the scene of the attack, and that I could sit up over the corpse and shoot the tiger.

While this information was being imparted to me, the girl followed my every movement with the liquid pleading eyes of a wounded animal. Room to move unhampered, quiet to collect my wits, and clean air for the girl to breathe, were necessary, and I am afraid the methods I employed to gain them were not as gentle as they might have been. When the last of the men had left in a hurry, I set the women to warming water and to tearing my shirt (which was comparatively dry) into bandages, while one was sent to scour the village for a pair of scissors. The water and bandages were ready, before the woman I had sent for a pair of scissors returned with the only pair the village could produce. They had been found in the house of a tailor (long since dead) and had been used for digging potatoes. The blades, being eight inches long, could not be made to meet at any point and after a vain attempt, I decided to leave the hair alone. The major wounds consisted of a cut, starting between the eyes and extending right over the head and down to the nape of the neck, laying the scalp in two halves. Another cut, starting near the first ran across the forehead up to the right ear. Besides these two wounds there were a number of skin deep scratches on the right breast, right shoulder and back, and one very deep cut on the back of the right hand, evidently inflicted when the girl had put up her hand in a vain attempt to shield her head.

A doctor friend, whom I had once taken out tiger shooting on foot had, after his brief visit, sent me a bottle of yellow fluid which he advised me to carry whenever I went into the jungles.

I had carried the bottle in my pocket for over a year, and a portion of the fluid had dried; but the bottle was still three parts full, and knocking off the neck I poured the fluid into the wounds, and after bandaging the head, to try to keep the scalp in position, I carried the girl home – a single room, combining living quarters, kitchen and nursery – with the women following me.

Dependent from the rafter was an open basket, the occupant of which was now clamouring to be fed. This was a complication with which I could not deal, so I left the solution of it to the assembled women. Ten days later when, on the eve of my departure, I visited the girl for the last time, I found her sitting on the door-step of her home with the baby asleep in her lap.

Her wounds, except for a sore at the nape of her neck, where the tiger's claw had sunk deepest into her flesh, were all healed and when parting her hair to shew me where the scalp had made a perfect join, she said, with a smile, that she was glad that her dear sister had – quite by mistake – borrowed the wrong pair of scissors from the tailor's widow. If these lines should ever be read by my friend the doctor I would like him to know that the little bottle of yellow fluid he so thoughtfully provided for me, had saved the life of a very brave young mother.

While I had been attending to the girl my men had procured a goat. Following the blood trail made by the girl I found the spot where the attack had been made, and tying the goat to a bush I climbed into a stunted oak, the only tree in the vicinity, and prepared for an all night vigil. Sleep, even in snatches, was not possible, for the branch I sat on was only a few feet from the ground, and the tigress was still without her dinner. However I neither heard nor saw anything throughout that night.

On examining the ground in the morning, I found that the tigress, after dragging the girl, had gone up the valley for half a mile to where a cattle track crossed the Nandhar River. This track it had followed for two miles, to its junction with the forest road on the ridge above Dalkania village. Here on the hard ground I lost the tracks.

For two days the people in all the surrounding villages kept as close to their habitations as the want of sanitary arrangments permitted, and then on the third day news was brought to me by four runners that the man-eater had claimed a victim at Lohali, a village five miles to the South of Dalkania. The runners stated that the distance by the forest road was ten miles, but only five by a short cut by which they proposed taking me back. My preparations were soon made and at mid-day I set off with my four guides.

A very stiff climb of two miles brought us to the crest of a long ridge south of Dalkania and in view of the valley three miles below where the "kill" was reported to have taken place. My guides could give me no particulars of the kill. They lived in a small village a mile on the near side of Lohali and at 10 a.m. a message had come to them – in the manner already described – that a woman of Lohali village had been killed by the man-eater and that they must immediately go to Dalkania and inform me.

The top of the hill on which we were standing was bare of trees, and while I regained my breath and had a smoke, my companions pointed out the land marks. Close to where we were sitting and under the shelter of a great rock there was a small ruined hut, with a circular thorn enclosure near by. Questioned about this hut, the men told me the following story. Three years previously a Bhootia (trans-border man) who had been packing goor, salt and other commodities all the winter from the bazaars at the foot-hills into the interior of the district had built the hut with the object of resting and fattening his flock of goats through the summer and rains and getting them fit for the next winter's work. After a few weeks, the goats wandered down the hill and damaged my informants' crops, and when they came up to lodge a protest, they found the hut empty, and the fierce sheep dog these men invariably keep with them to guard their camps at night, chained to an iron stake and dead. Foul play was suspected and next day men were collected from adjoining villages and a search organised. Pointing to an oak tree scored by lightning and distant some four hundred yards, my informants said that under it the remains of the man – his skull and a few splinters of bone – and his clothes had been found. This was the Chowgarh man-eater's first human victim.

There was no way of descending the precipitous hill from where we were sitting, and the men informed me we should have to proceed half a mile along the ridge, to where we should find a very steep and rough track, which would take us straight down to the valley below. We had covered about half the distance we had to go along the ridge, when all at once, and without being able to ascribe any reason for it, I felt we were being followed. Arguing with myself against this feeling was of no avail, and as we were now at the widest part of the grassy ridge, I made the men sit down, instructed them they were not to move until I returned and set off on a tour of investigation. Retracing my steps to where we had first come out on the ridge, I entered the jungle, and carefully worked round the open ground and back to where the men were sitting. No alarm call of animal or bird indicated that a tiger was anywhere in the vicinity, but from there on I made the four men walk in front of me, while I brought up the rear, with thumb on safety catch and a constant look out behind. Arrived at the little village my companions had started from, they asked for permission to leave me. I was very glad of this request. I had still to go a mile through very thick scrub, and though the feeling of uneasiness had long since left me, I felt safer and more comfortable with only my own life to guard. A little below the out-lying terraced fields, where the thick scrub started, there was a spring of cool crystal clear water, from which the village evidently drew its water supply. Here in the wet soft ground I found the fresh pug marks of the man-eater.

These pug marks, which pointed up hill, coupled with the uneasy feeling I had experienced on the ridge above, convinced me that something had gone wrong with the "kill" and that my quest would be fruitless. As I emerged from the scrub jungle I came in view of Lohali village, which consisted of five or six houses. Near the door of one of them, a group of people were collected.

My approach over the steep open ground and narrow terraced fields was observed, and a few men detached themselves from the group near the door and advanced to meet me. One of the number, an old man, bent down to touch my feet, and with tears streaming down his cheeks implored me to save the life of his daughter. His story was as short as it was tragic. His daughter, who was a widow and the only relation he had in the world, had gone out at about ten o'clock to collect dry sticks, with which to cook their mid-day meal. A small stream flowed through the valley and on the far side of the stream the hill went steeply up. On the lower slope of the hill were a few terraced fields. At the edge of the lowest field distant about 150 yards from her home the woman had started to collect sticks. A little later some women who were washing their clothes in the stream, heard a scream; and on looking up, saw the woman and tiger disappearing together into the dense thorn bushes which extended from the edge of the field, right down to the stream. Dashing back to the village the women raised an alarm. The frightened villagers made no attempt at a rescue, but a message for help was shouted to a village higher up the valley, from where it was tossed back to the village from which the four men had set out to find me.

Half an hour after the message had been sent the wounded woman crawled home. Her story was that she had seen the tiger just as it was about to spring on her, and as there was no time to run, she had jumped down an almost perpendicular hill side and while she was in the air the tiger had caught her and they had gone down together. She remembered nothing further until she regained consciousness and found herself at the bottom of the ravine; and being unble to call for help, she had crawled back to the village. We had reached the door of the house while this tale was being told. Making the people stand back from the door – the only opening in the four walls of the room –

I drew the blood-stained sheet off the woman. Had I been a qualified doctor, armed with modern appliances, instead of just a mere man with a little permanganate of potach in his pocket, I do not think it would have been possible to do anything for the woman. The deep claw and tooth wounds in her neck and on her face had, in that hot unventilated room, turned septic. Mercifully she was only semi-conscious. The father had followed me into the room, and more for his satisfaction than for any good I thought it would do, I washed the caked blood from the woman's head and body and cleaned out the wounds as best I could, with my handkerchief and a strong solution of permanganate.

It was now too late to think of returning to my camp, and a place would have to be found in which to pass the night. A little way up the stream, and not far from where the women had been washing their clothes, there was a great Pepal tree, with a masonry platform round it, used by the villagers for religious ceremonies.

Undressing on the platform, I bathed in the stream, and when the wind had carried out the functions of a towel, dressed again; and with my back to the tree and the loaded rifle laid by my side, prepared to see the night out. Admittedly, it was an unsuitable place in which to pass the night, but any place was better than the village and that dark room, with its hot fetid atmosphere and swarm of buzzing flies, where a woman fought for breath.

During the night the wailing of women announced that the sufferer's troubles were over and when I passed through the village at day-break, preparations for the funeral were well advanced.

I stayed at Dalkania for another week and announced on Saturday that I would start for home the following Monday. I had now been in the man-eater's domain for close on a month and the constant strain of sleeping in an open tent, and walking endless miles during the day, with the prospect of every step being the last, was beginning to tell on my nerves. The villagers received my announcement with consternation, and only desisted from trying to make me change my decision when I promised to return at the first opportunity. After breakfast on Sunday morning the head-men paid me a visit and requested me to shoot them some game before I left. The request was gladly acceded to, and half an hour later, accompanied by four villagers and one of my own men and armed with a .275 rifle and a clip of cartridges, I set off for the hill on the far side of the Nandhar river, on the upper slopes of which I had, from my camp, frequently seen Ghooral feeding.

One of the villagers accompanying me was a tall gaunt man with a terribly disfigured face. He had been a constant visitor to my camp, and finding in me a good listener, had told and retold his encounter with the man-eater so often, that I could without effort repeat the whole story in my sleep. The encounter had taken place four years previously and is best described in his words.

"Do you see that pine tree, sahib, at the bottom of the grassy slope on the shoulder of the hill – yes, the pine tree with a big white rock to the East of it – well it was at the upper end of the grassy slope that the tiger attacked me. The grassy slope is as perpendicular as the wall of a house, and none but a hill man could put foot on it. My son, who was eight years of age at the time, and I, had cut grass on the day of my misfortune, carrying the grass up in armfuls to the belt of trees where the ground is level. I was stooping down at the very edge of the slope, tying the grass into a big bundle, when the tiger sprang at me and buried his teeth, one under my right eye, one in my chin and the other two here at the back of my neck. The tiger's mouth struck me with a great blow and I fell over on my back, while the tiger lay on top of me chest to chest, and his stomach between my legs. When falling backwards I had flung out my arms and my right had come in contact with an oak sapling. As my fingers grasped the sapling, an idea came to me. My legs were free and if I could draw them up and get my feet against the tiger's belly, I might be able to push the tiger off and run away. The pain, as the tiger crushed all the bones on the right side of my face, was terrible; but I did not lose consciousness, for you see sahib, at that time I was a young man, and in all the hills there was no man to compare with me in strength. Very slowly, so as not to anger the tiger, I drew my legs up on either side of it, and gently, very gently, inserted my feet against its belly. Then placing my left hand against its chest and pushing and kicking upwards with all my might, I lifted the tiger right off me and we being on the very edge of the perpendicular hill-side, the tiger went crashing down and belike would have taken me with him, had my hold on the sapling not been a good one. My son had been too frightened to run away, and when the tiger had gone, I took his loin cloth from him and wrapping it round my head and holding his hand I walked back to the village. Arrived at home I told my wife to call all my friends together, for I wished to see their faces before I died. When my friends were assembled and saw my condition, they wanted to put me on a charpai and carry me fifty miles to the Almora hospital, but this I would not consent to, for my suffering was great, and being assured that my time had come, I wanted to die where I had been born, and where I had lived all my life. Water was brought, for I was thirsty and my head was on fire, but when it was poured into my mouth, it all flowed out through the holes in my neck. Thereafter there was great confusion in my mind and much pain in my face and while I waited to die, my wounds healed and I became well. And now sahib I am as you see me, old and thin, and with white hair, and a face that no man can look on without repulsion. My enemy lives and continues to claim victims; but do not be deceived into thinking it is a tiger, for it is no tiger but an evil spirit, who, when it craves for human blood and flesh, takes on for a little time the semblance of a tiger. But they say you are a sadhu sahib, and the spirits that guard sadhus are more powerful than this evil spirit, as is proved by the fact that you lived three days and nights alone in the jungle, and came out alive and unhurt."

Looking at the great frame of the man, it was easy to picture him as having been a giant of a man. And a giant in strength he must have been, for no man, unless he was gifted with strength far above the average, could have lifted the tiger into the air, torn its hold from the side of his head, carrying away, as it did, half his face with it, and hurled it down the steep hill-side.

My gaunt friend constituted himself our leader, and with a beautifully polished axe, with long tapering handle, over his shoulder, led us by devious steep paths to the valley below.

Fording the shallow river, we crossed several wide terraced fields now gone out of cultivation for fear of the man-eater, and reaching the foot of the hill, started what proved to be a very stiff climb, through forest to the grass slopes above. Gaunt our leader may have been, but he lacked nothing in wind, and tough as I was, it was only by frequent halts – to admire the view – that I was able to keep up with him.

Emerging from the tree forest, we went diagonally across the grassy slope, in the direction of a rock cliff that extended upwards for a thousand feet or more. It was on this cliff, sprinkled over with tufts of grass, that I had seen ghooral feeding from my tent. We had covered a few hundred yards when a ghooral started up out of a small ravine, and at my shot, crumpled up, and slipped back out of sight. Alarmed by the report of the rifle, another ghooral, that had evidently been lying asleep at the foot of the cliff, sprang to his feet and went up the rock face, as only he or his big brother the Tahr could have done. As he climbed upwards, I lay down and putting the sight to 200 yards, waited for him to stop. This he presently did, coming out on a projecting rock to look down on us. At my shot he staggered, regained his footing and very slowly continued his climb. At the second shot he fell, hung for a second on a narrow ledge and then fell through space to the grassy slope from whence he had started. Striking the slope he rolled over and over, passing within a hundred yards of us, and eventually came to rest on a cattle track a hundred and fifty yards below.

I had only once in the years I have been shooting, witnessed a similar sight to the one we saw during the next few minutes, and in that case the marauder was a leopard.

The ghooral had hardly come to rest, before a bear came shuffling out of a deep ravine and without pause or stop came straight along the cattle track, covering a hundred yards of open ground, and stopped dead on reaching the ghooral. Sitting down on the track, it took the ghooral into its lap and as it started to nose it, I fired. May be I hurried over my shot; any way the bullet went low and struck the bear in the stomach. To the six of us who were intently watching, it appeared that the bear took the smack of the bullet as an assault from the ghooral, for, rearing up, he flung the dead animal from him and came lumbering along the track, emitting angry grunts. As he passed a hundred yards below I fired my fifth and last shot, the bullet going through the fleshy part of his hind legs. Descending the hill I examined the blood track, while the men recovered the ghooral. The track shewed the bear to be hard hit, but even so there was danger in following up with an empty rifle. A short council of war was held. Camp was three and a half miles away and as it was now 2 p.m., it would not be possible to fetch more ammunition, track down the bear and get home by dark, so it was unanimously decided that we should follow up the bear and try to finish it off with stones and axe. The hill was steep and fairly free of undergrowth and by keeping above the wounded animal there was a sporting chance of our being able to accomplish our task without mishap. We accordingly set off, I leading the way followed by three men, the rear being brought up by two men, each with a ghooral strapped to his back. Arrived at the spot where I had fired my second shot at the bear, additional blood on the track greatly encouraged us. A short distance further on, the blood track led down into a deep ravine. Here we divided up our force, two men crossing the ravine to the far side, the owner of the axe and I remaining on the near side, with the men carrying the ghooral following in our rear. On the word being given we started to advance down the hill. In the bed of the ravine and fifty feet below us was a thick patch of stunted bamboo. On a stone being thrown into this thicket, the bear got up with a roar and six men putting their best foot foremost went straight up the hill. I was not trained to this exercise, and on looking back, to see if the bear was gaining on us, I saw, much to my relief that he was going as hard down hill, as we were going up hill. A shout to my companions, a rapid change of direction, and we were off in full cry and rapidly gaining on our quarry. A few well aimed shots had been registered, followed by delighted shouts from the marksmen, and angry grunts from the bear, when at a sharp turn in the ravine, which necessitated a cautious advance, we lost the bear. To have followed the blood track would have been easy, but here the ravine was full of big rocks, behind any of which the bear might have been lurking, so while the encumbered men sat down for a rest, a cast was made on either side of the ravine. While my companion went forward to inspect the ravine I went to the right to look over a rocky crag that went sheer down for some two hundred feet. Holding to a tree for support I leaned over and saw the bear lying on a narrow ledge forty feet immediately below me. Stepping back I picked up a stone, about thirty pounds in weight and again advancing to the edge, in imminent danger of going over myself, raised the stone above my head with both hands, and hurled it at the bear.

The stone struck the ledge within a few inches of the bear's head, and scrambling to his feet, he disappeared from sight to reappear a minute later, on the side of the hill. Once again the hunt was on. The ground was now more open and less encumbered with rocks and the four of us who were running light had no difficulty in keeping up with him. For a mile we ran him until we eventually cleared the forest and emerged on to the terraced fields. Rain water had cut several narrow channels across these fields and in one of these channels the bear came to rest.

The man with the distorted face was the only armed member of the party and he was unanimously elected executioner. Nothing loth, he cautiously approached the bear, and swinging his beautifully polished axe aloft, brought the square head down on the bear's skull. The result was as alarming as it was unexpected. The axe head bounded off the bear's skull, as though it had been struck on a block of rubber, and with a scream of rage the bear reared up on his hind legs. Fortunately he did not follow up his advantage, for we were bunched together and in trying to run, got in each other's way.

The bear did not appear to like this open ground, and after going a short way down the channel, again came to rest. It was now my turn for the axe. The bear, however having once been struck, resented my approach, and it was only after a great deal of manoeuvring that I eventually got within striking distance. I had no fear, as the owner had, of the axe glancing off and getting damaged on the stones, and the moment I got within reach I buried the entire blade in his skull.

Himalayan bear skins are very greatly prized by our hill folk, and the owner of the axe was a very proud and envied man when I told him that he could have the skin, in addition to his share of the ghooral. Leaving the men, whose numbers were being rapidly augmented by new arrivals from the village, to skin and divide up the bag, I climbed up to the village and paid, as already related, a last visit to the injured girl. The day had been a very strenuous one, and if the man-eater had paid me a visit that night, he would have "caught me napping".

On the road I had taken when coming to Dalkania there were several long stiff climbs up tree-less hills, and when mentioning the discomforts of the road to the villagers, they had suggested that I should go via Haira Khan. This route would necessitate only one climb, to the ridge above the village, from where it was downhill all the way to Ranibagh, whence I could complete the journey by car.

I had warned my men overnight to prepare for an early start, and a little before sunrise, leaving them to pack up and follow me, I started on the two mile climb to the Forest road on the ridge above. The footpath I took was not the one by which my men, and later I, had arrived at Dalkania, but was one the villagers used when going to and from the bazaars at the foot-hills.

The path wound in and out of deep ravines, through thick oak and pine forests and dense undergrowth. There had been no news of the tigress for a week. However, this absence of news made me all the more careful, and an hour after leaving camp I arrived without mishap at an open glade near the top of the hill, and within a hundred yards of the Forest Road.

The glade was pear-shaped, roughly a hundred yards long by fifty yards wide, with a stagnant pool of rain water in the centre of it. Sambhar used this pool as a wallow; and curious to see the tracks round it, I left the path which skirted the left hand side of the glade, passing close under a cliff of rock which extended up to the forest road. As I approached the pool I saw the pug marks of the tigress in the soft earth at the edge of the water. She had approached the pool from the same side as I had, and evidently disturbed by me, had crossed the water and then the glade and gone into the dense tree and scrub jungle on the right hand side of the glade. A great chance lost, for had I kept as careful a look out in front as I had behind, I would have seen her before she saw me. However, though I had missed a chance, the advantages were now all on my side. The tigress had seen me, or she would not have crossed the pool and hurried for shelter as her tracks shewed she had done. Having seen me, she had also seen that I was alone and watching me now from cover as she undoubtedly was, she would assume I was going to the pool to drink as she had done. My movements up to this had been quite natural, and if I could continue to make her think I was unaware of her presence, she would possibly give me a second chance. Stooping down and keeping a very sharp lookout from under my hat, I coughed several times, splashed the water about and then very slowly gathering dry sticks on the way I went to the foot of the steep rock. Here I built a small fire, and putting my back to the rock lit a cigarette. By the time the cigarette had been smoked the fire had burnt out. I now lay down and pillowing my head on my left arm, placed the rifle on the ground with my finger on the trigger. The rock above me was too steep for any animal to climb, I had therefore only my front to guard, and as the heavy cover nowhere approached to within less than twenty yards of my position, I was quite safe. I had all this time neither seen nor heard anything; nevertheless I was convinced that the tigress was watching me. The rim of my hat, while effectually shading my eyes, did not obstruct my vision, and inch by inch I scanned every bit of the jungle within my view. There was not a breath of wind, and not a leaf or blade of grass stirred. My men, whom I had instructed to keep close together and sing from the time they left camp until they joined me on the forest road, were not due for an hour and a half, and during this time it was more than likely that the tigress would break cover and try and stalk me. There are occasions when time drags, and others when time flies. My left arm, on which my head was pillowed, had long since ceased to prick and had gone dead, but even so the singing of the men in the valley below reached me all to soon. The voices grew louder and presently I caught sight of them as they rounded a sharp bend. It was possible at this bend that the tigress had seen me as she turned round to retrace her steps after having her drink. Another failure, and the last chance on this trip gone. After my men had rested we climbed up to the Forest road, and set off on what proved to be a very long twenty mile march to the Forest Rest House at Haira Khan. The road, after going a couple of hundred yards over open ground, entered very thick forest. Here I made the men walk in front of me while I brought up the rear. We had gone about two miles in this order, when on turning a corner I saw a man sitting on the side of the road, herding buffaloes. It was now time to call a halt for breakfast, and on my asking the man where we could get water, he pointed down the hill straight in front of him, and said there was a spring down there, from which his village, which was just round the shoulder of the hill, drew its water supply. There was however, he said, no necessity for us to go down the hill for water, for if we continued a little further we would find a good spring on the road.

His village was at the upper end of the valley in which the woman had been killed a week previously, and he told me that nothing had been heard of the man-eater since, and that the animal was possibly now at the other end of the district. I disabused his mind on this point by telling him about the pug marks I had seen, and advised him very strongly to collect his buffaloes and return to the village. His buffaloes, some ten in number, were straggling towards the road and he said he would leave as soon as they had grazed up to the road. Handing him a cigarette I left him with a final warning. What followed was related to me by the men of his village when I paid the district a second visit some months later.

He told them he watched me go round a bend in the road a hundred yards away and that he then began to light his cigarette. A wind was blowing, and to protect the flame of the match he bent forward, and while in this position, he was seized by the right shoulder and pulled backwards. His first thought was of the party who had just left him, but unfortunately his cry for help was not heard by them. Help however was nearer at hand, for as soon as the buffaloes heard his cry, mingled with the growl of the tigress, they charged on to the road and drove the tigress off. His shoulder and arm were broken, and with great difficulty he managed to climb on the back of a buffalo, and followed by the rest of the herd, reached the village. The villagers tied up his wounds as best they could and carried him thirty miles to the Haldwani hospital, where he died soon after admission.

When Atropos who snips the threads of life misses one thread she cuts another, and we who do not know why one thread is missed and another cut, call it Fate, Kismat, or what we will.

For a month and more the man-eater had missed many golden opportunities and now when making a final effort had, quite by chance, encountered this unfortunate man and claimed him as a victim.

CHAPTER II

The following February I returned to Dalkania. Several human beings had been killed over a wide area in the interval, and as the whereabouts of the tigress were not known and the chances in one place were as good as in another, I decided to return and camp on the ground with which I was now familiar.

On my arrival at Dalkania I was told that a cow had been killed the previous evening, on the hill on which the bear hunt had taken place. The men who had been herding the cattle at the time were positive that the animal they had seen killing the cow, was a tiger. The kill was lying near some bushes at the edge of a deserted field, and was clearly visible from the spot where my tent was being put up. Vultures were circling over the kill and on looking through my field-glasses, I saw several of these birds, perched on a tree, to the left of the kill. From the fact that the kill was lying out in the open, and the vultures had not descended on it, I concluded (a) that the cow had been killed by a leopard and (b) that the leopard was lying up close to the kill.

The ground below the field on which the cow was lying was very steep and overgrown with dense brushwood. The man-eater was still at large, and an approach over this ground was therefore inadvisable.

To the right was a grassy slope but the ground here was too open to admit of my approaching the kill without being seen. A deep heavily wooded ravine, starting from near the crest of the hill, ran right down to the Nandhar river, passing within a short distance of the kill. The tree on which the vultures were perched was growing on the edge of this ravine. I decided on this ravine as my line of approach. While I had been planning out the stalk with the assistance of the villagers, who knew every foot of the ground, my men had prepared tea for me. The day was by now on the decline, but by going hard I would just have time to visit the kill, and return to camp before night-fall.

Before setting off I instructed my men to be on the look out, and if after hearing a shot, they saw me on the open ground near the kill three or four of them were immediately to leave camp, and keeping to the open grassy slope, join me at the kill. On the other hand if I did not fire, and failed to return by morning, a search party was to be organised.

The ravine was overgrown with raspberry bushes and strewn with great rocks, and as the wind was blowing down hill, my progress was of necessity slow. I reached the tree on which the vultures were perched, only to find that the kill was not visible from this spot. The deserted field, which through my field glasses had appeared to be quite straight, I found to be crescent shaped, ten yards across at its widest part and tapering to a point at both ends. The outer edge was bordered with dense undergrowth, and the hill fell steeply away from the inner edge. Two thirds of the field was visible from where I was standing and in order to see the remaining one third, on which the kill was lying, it would be necessary, either to make a wide detour and approach from the far side, or climb the tree on which the vultures were perched.

I decided on the latter course. The cow, as far as I could judge, was about twenty yards from the tree, and it was quite possible that the animal that had killed her was even less than that distance from me. To climb the tree without disturbing the killer would have been an impossible feat, and would not have been attempted, had it not been for the vultures. There were by now some twenty of these birds on the tree and their number was being added to by new arrivals, and as the accommodation in the upper branches was limited, there was much flapping of wings and quarrelling. The tree was leaning outwards away from the hill, and about ten feet from the ground a great limb projected out over the steep hill-side. Hampered with the rifle, I had great difficulty in reaching the limb. Waiting until a fresh quarrel had broken out among the vultures, I stepped out along the limb – a difficult balancing feat where a slip or false step would have resulted in a fall of a hundred or more feet, on to the rocks below – and reaching a fork in the branch, sat down.

The kill, from which only a few pounds of flesh had been eaten, was now in full view. I had been in position about ten minutes, and was finding my perch none too comfortable when two vultures who had been circling round and were uncertain of their welcome on the tree, alighted on the field a short distance from the kill. They had hardly come to rest, when they were on the wing again and at the same moment the bushes on my side of the kill were gently agitated and out into the open stepped a fine male leopard.

Those who have never seen a leopard under favourable conditions in his natural surroundings, can have no conception of the grace of movement and beauty of colouring of this, the most graceful and most beautiful of all the animals of our jungles. Nor are his attractions limited to outward appearances, for pound for pound, his strength is second to none, and in courage he lacks nothing. To class such an animal as VERMIN, as is done in some parts of India, is a crime which only those could perpetrate whose knowledge of the leopard is limited to the miserable, underfed, mangy specimens seen in captivity.

But beautiful as the specimen was that stood before me, his life was forfeit, for he had taken to cattle killing – possibly because of stress of circumstances – and I had promised the villagers on my last visit that I would rid them of this their minor enemy, if opportunity offered. The opportunity had come and I do not think the leopard heard the shot that killed him.

Of the many incomprehensible things one meets in life, the hardest to assign any reason for is the way in which misfortune dogs an individual or a family. Take as an example the case of the owner of the cow over which I had shot the leopard.

He was a boy, eight years of age and an only child. Two years previously his mother, while out gathering grass for the cow, had been killed and eaten by the man-eater, and twelve months later his father had suffered a like fate. The few pots and pans the family possessed had been sold to pay off the small debt left by the father, and the son started life as the owner of one cow; and this particular cow the leopard had selected out of a herd of two or three hundred head of village cattle, and killed.

My young buffaloes had been well cared for by the man in whose charge I had left them, and the day after my arrival I started tying them out, though I had little hope of the tigress accepting them as bait.

Five miles down the Nandhar valley nestles a little village at the foot of a great crag of rock, some thousand or more feet high. The man-eater had, during the past few months, killed four people on the outskirts of this village. Shortly after I had shot the leopard, a deputation came from this village to request me to move my camp from Dalkania to a site they had selected near their village. I was told that the tiger had frequently been seen on the rocks above the village and that it evidently had its home in one of the big caves in the rock face. That very morning some women out cutting grass had seen the tiger, and the villagers were now in a state of terror, and were frightened to leave their homes. Promising the deputation I would do all I could to help them, I made a very early start next morning, climbed the hill opposite the village, and scanned the rocks for an hour or more through my field-glasses. I then crossed the valley, and going up a very deep ravine, climbed the crags above the village. Here the going was very difficult and not at all to my liking, for added to the danger of a fall, which would have resulted in a broken neck, was the danger of an attack on ground on which it would be impossible to defend oneself. By 2 p.m. I had seen as much of the rocks as I shall ever want to see again, and was making my way up the valley towards my camp and breakfast, when on looking back before starting the stiff climb to my camp, I saw two men running towards me from the direction in which I had just come. On joining me, the men said that the tiger had just killed a bullock in the deep ravine up which I had gone earlier in the day. Telling one of the men to go on up to my camp and instruct my servant to send tea and food for me, I turned round and accompanied by the other man, retraced my steps down the valley. The ravine where the bullock had been killed was about two hundred feet deep, one hundred feet wide and about one hundred yards from the village. As we approached the ravine I saw a number of vultures rising out of it, and on arrival at the kill I found that the vultures had cleaned out the bullock, leaving only the skin and bones. Leaving the ravine by the way we had entered it, we took a cattle path which wound in and out of dense scrub to the village. Here I explained to the head-man that the kill had been spoiled by the vultures, and that as it would take too long to send to Dalkania for one of my buffaloes, he must provide a young buffalo for me, also a length of stout rope. While these were being fetched, two of my men arrived with the tea and food I had sent for. The sun was near setting when I re-entered the ravine, followed by several men leading the buffalo. Fifty yards above where the bullock had been killed, one end of a pine tree washed down from the hill above, had been buried deep in the bed of the ravine. To the exposed end of the tree the buffalo was securely fastened, after which the men returned to the village. There were no trees in the ravine and the only place for me to sit up, was a narrow ledge on the side of the ravine nearest the village, so with great difficulty I climbed to the ledge which was about two feet wide by five feet long, and twenty feet above the bed of the ravine. From a little below the ledge the rock shelved inwards, forming a deep recess that was not visible from the ledge. When I had taken my seat on the cold hard ledge, with my right shoulder pressed against the hill to retain my balance, my back was toward the direction in which I expected the tiger to come, while the tethered buffalo was to my left front and distant about thirty yards from me.

The sun had set when the buffalo, which had been lying down, scrambled to his feet and faced up the ravine. A moment later a stone came rolling down. To have turned my head would have been to risk a fall, with the possibility of broken bones and the certainty of giving the man-eater an easy meal. After some time the buffalo gradually turned round until he was facing in my direction. This shewed that whatever he was frightened of, was now in the recess below me. Presently the head of a tiger appeared directly under me. I have no fancy for firing at tiger heads, and further any movement on my part might have betrayed my presence. For a long minute or two, during which my heart missed several beats, the head remained perfectly still, and then with two great bounds the tiger was on the buffalo. There was no struggle and no sound, beyond the impact of the two heavy bodies, after which the buffalo lay quite still with the tiger lying partly over it and holding it by the throat. It is generally believed that tigers kill by delivering a smashing blow on the neck. If nature had intended this to be the tiger's method of killing, she would have provided them with knuckle dusters in place of soft pads.

The right side of the tiger was towards me, and taking very careful aim with the .275 I had armed myself with when leaving camp that morning, I fired. Relinquishing its hold on the buffalo, the tiger, without making a sound, turned and bounded off up the ravine and out of sight. Clearly a miss, which I was unable to assign any reason for. If the tiger had not seen me or the flash of the rifle it was just possible it would return; so recharging the rifle as silently as I could, I sat on.

The buffalo, after the tiger left him, lay without movement, and the conviction grew on me that I had shot him instead of the tiger. Ten – fifteen minutes – dragged by, when the tiger's head for a second time, appeared from the recess below me. Again there was a long pause and then, very slowly, the tiger emerged and walking up to the buffalo stood looking down at it. With the whole length of the back as a target I was going to make no mistake the second time. Very carefully the sights were aligned, and the trigger slowly pressed; but – instead of the tiger falling dead as I expected it to – it sprang to the left and went tearing up a little side ravine, dislodging stones as it went up the steep hill side. Two shots fired at a range of thirty yards, and heard by anxious villagers for miles round: and all I would have to show for them would be, certainly, and quite possibly two, bullet holes in a dead buffalo. Clearly my eyesight was failing or (comforting thought), in climbing the rock I had knocked the foresight out of alignment, but a glance along the barrel shewed there was nothing wrong with the rifle, so it was my eyes without question that were at fault.

There was no chance of the tiger returning a third time; and even if it did return, there was nothing to be gained by risking a shot in uncertain light when I had not been able to hit it while the light had been good. Under these circumstances to remain longer on the ledge was useless.

My clothes were still damp from hill climbing, a cold wind was blowing and promised to get colder, my shorts were thin and the rock was hard and cold, and a hot cup of tea awaited me in the village. Good as these reasons were, there was a better and more convincing reason for my remaining where I was – the man-eater. It was now dark. A quarter of a mile walk along a boulder-stewn ravine and a winding path bordered by dense undergrowth lay between me and the village. I had received no definite news of the man-eater, nor had I seen her pug marks since my arrival; and though she might at that moment have been fifty miles away, she might also have been watching from a distance of fifty yards, so uncomfortable as my perch was, prudence dictated that I should remain where I was. As the long hours dragged by, the conviction grew on me that man-eater shooting by night was not a pastime that appealed to me, and that if the animal could not be shot during daylight hours she would have to be left to die of old age. This conviction was strengthened, when, cold and stiff, I started to climb down as soon as there was sufficient light to shoot by, and slipping on the dew-drenched rock completed my descent with my feet in the air. Fortunately, I landed on a bed of sand, without doing myself or the rifle any injury. Early as it was

I found the village astir, and in reply to the eager questions that met me on all sides, I was only able to say that I had been firing at a Phantom tiger with blank ammunition.

A fire, and a hot drink, did much to restore warmth to my outer and inner man, and accompanied by most of the men folk of the village, I went back to a great slab of rock that jutted out over the ravine and overlooked the scene of my overnight exploit. To the assembled men I explained how the tiger had appeared from the recess-like cave under me and had bounded on to the buffalo. I had fired and it had gone in THAT direction, and as I pointed up the ravine there was a shout of, "Look sahib, there is the tiger lying dead." My eyes were strained with an all-night vigil, but even after looking away and back again there was no denying the fact that the tiger was lying there, dead. To the very natural question of why I had fired a second shot after a period of ten minutes, I answered that the tiger had appeared a second time from exactly the same place, and that I had fired at it while it was standing near the buffalo, and that it had gone up THAT side ravine – and again there was a shout of, "Look sahib, there is another tiger lying dead." Both tigers were lying within sixty yards of where I had fired at them, and both had evidently died in their tracks, for neither had made a sound. As far as could be seen from the projecting rock, both tigers appeared to be about the same size.

Questioned on the subject of this second tiger the villagers said that when the four human beings had been killed only one tiger had been seen, and also on the previous day only one tiger had been seen when the bullock was killed. The mating season for tigers is an elastic one extending from November to April, and the man-eater – if either of the two tigers was the man-eater – had evidently provided herself with a mate.

A way into the ravine, down the steep rock face, was found some two hundred yards below where I had sat up, and followed by the entire population of the village, I went past the dead buffalo to where the first tiger was lying. As I approached it hope rose high, for she was an old tigress. Handing the rifle to the nearest man I got down on my knees to examine her feet. On that day when the tigress had tried to stalk the women cutting wheat, she had left some beautiful pug marks on the edge of the field. They were the first pug marks I had seen of the man-eater, and I had examined them very carefully. They shewed the tigress to be a very old animal, whose feet had splayed out with age. The pads of the fore feet were heavily rutted, one deep rut running right across the pad of the right fore foot, and the toes were elongated to a length I had never before seen in a tiger. With these distinctive feet it would have been easy to pick the man-eater out of a hundred dead tigers. The animal before me was, I found to my great regret, not the man-eater. When I said so to the assembled crowd there was a murmur of strong dissent from all sides. They asserted that I myself had, on my first visit, declared the man-eater to be an old tigress, and such an animal I had now shot, a few yards from where, only a short while previously, four of their number had been killed. Against this convincing evidence, of what value was the evidence of the feet, for the feet of all tigers were alike!

The second tiger could, under the circumstances, only be a

male, and while I made preparations to skin the tigress I sent the villagers to fetch him. The side ravine was steep and narrow, and after a great deal of shouting and laughter the second tiger – a fine male – was laid down alongside the tigress.

The skinning of those two tigers, that had been dead fourteen hours, with the sun beating down on my back, and with an ever growing crowd of men, women and children, was one of the most unpleasant tasks I have ever undertaken.

By early afternoon the job was completed and with the skins neatly tied up for my men to carry, I was ready to start on my five-mile walk back to camp.

During the morning, head men and others had come in from adjoining villages, and before leaving I assured them that the man-eater of CHOWGARH was not dead and warned them that the slackening of precautions would give the tigress the opportunity she was waiting for. Had my warnings been heeded, the man-eater would not have claimed as many victims as she did, during the succeeding months.

There was no further news of the man-eater, and after a stay of three weeks in Dalkania, I left to keep an appointment with the district officials in the Tarai.

CHAPTER III

In March 1930 Mr Vivian, our District Commissioner was touring through the man-eater's domain, and on the 22nd of the month I received an urgent request from him to go to Kala Agar, where he said he would await my arrival. It is roughly fifty miles from Naini Tal to Kala Agar, and on the second day after receipt of his letter, I arrived in time for breakfast, at the Kala Agar Forest Bungalow, where he and Mrs Vivian were staying.

Over breakfast the Vivians told me they had arrived at the bungalow on the afternoon of the 21st, and while they were having tea in the verandah, one of six women, who were cutting grass close to the bungalow, had been killed and carried off by the man eater. Rifles were hurriedly seized, and accompanied by several of his staff, Mr Vivian followed up the "drag" and found the dead woman tucked away under a bush at the foot of an oak tree. On the approach of the party the tigress had gone off down the hill-side and all through the subsequent proceedings she had sheltered in a deep ravine a hundred yards from the kill. A machan was put up in the oak tree for Mr Vivian, and two others in trees along the forest road, which passed thirty yards above the kill, for members of his staff. The machans were occupied as soon as they were ready and the party sat up the whole night, without however seeing anything of the tigress.

Next morning the body of the woman was removed for cremation, and a young buffalo was tied up on the forest road and killed by the tigress the same night. The following evening both Mr and Mrs Vivian sat up over the buffalo and just as it was getting dark saw an animal approach the kill, which they unfortunately mistook for a bear. Later when examining the ground, I found they had mistaken the tigress for a bear and so after a very sporting effort, lost an opportunity of bagging the man-eater.

On the 25th, the Vivians left Kala Agar and during the course of the day my buffaloes arrived from Dalkania. As the tigress now appeared to be inclined to accept this form of bait I tied up the four buffaloes, at intervals of a few hundred yards, along the forest road. For three nights the tigress passed within a few feet of the buffaloes without however touching them; but on the fourth, the buffalo nearest the bungalow was killed. On examining the kill in the morning I was disappointed to find that the buffalo had been killed by a pair of leopards that I had heard calling the previous night, above the bungalow. I did not like firing in this locality for fear of driving away the tigress, but it was quite evident that if I did not shoot the leopards, they woul kill my three remaining buffaloes, so I followed up the leopards and shot them. The forest road from Kala Agar bungalow runs for several miles due West through very beautiful forests of pine, oak, and rhododendron, and in these forests there is, compared with the rest of Kumaon, quite a lot of game in the way of sambhar, karker and pig. On two occasions I suspected the tigress of having killed sambhar, and though on both occasions I found a little blood, I failed to find either of the kills.

For the next fourteen days I spent all the daylight hours either on the forest road or in the jungles, and only twice during that period did I get near the tigress. I had on the first occasion been down to an isolated village, on the South East face of the ridge, that had been abandoned the previous year on account of the depredations of the man eater, and had taken a cattle track, which went over the ridge and down the far side to the forest road, when on approaching a pile of rocks, I suddenly felt there was danger ahead. The distance from the ridge to the forest road was roughly three hundred yards. The track for a few yards went steeply down, then turned to the right and ran diagonally across the hill for a hundred yards. The pile of rocks was about midway on the right hand side of this length of the track. Beyond the rocks a hairpin bend carried the track to the left and a hundred yards further on another sharp bend took it down to its junction with the forest road. I had been along this track many times and this was the first occasion on which I hesitated to pass the rocks. To avoid the rocks I would either have had to go several hundred yards through dense undergrowth, or make a wide detour round and above the rocks. The former would have subjected me to very grave danger, and as the sun was near setting and I had still two miles to go, there was no time for the latter. So, whether I liked it or not, there was nothing for it but to face the rocks. The wind was blowing up the hill so I was able to ignore the thick cover on the left of the track, and concentrate on the rocks to the right. A hundred feet would see me clear of the danger zone and this distance I covered foot by foot, walking sideways with my face to the rocks and the rifle to my shoulder. A strange mode of progression, had there been any to see it.

Thirty yards beyond the rocks was an open glade running up the hill and screened from the rocks by a fringe of bushes, and in this glade a karker was grazing. I saw her before she saw me, and turning my head, watched her out of the corner of my eye. On catching sight of me she threw up her head, and as I was not looking in her direction, but was moving steadily on she stood stock still, as these animals have a habit of doing when they are under the impression they have not been observed. Arrived at the hairpin bend, I looked over my shoulder and saw that the karker had lowered her head and was once more cropping grass.

I had walked a short distance along the track after passing the bend when the karker went dashing up the hill, barking hysterically. In a few quick strides I was back at the bend, and was just in time to see a movement in the bushes on the lower side of the track. That the karker had seen the tigress was quite evident and the only place where she could have seen her was on the track. The movement I had seen might have been caused by the passage of a bird, but in any case an investigation was necessary before going further on my way.

A trickle of water seeping out from under the rocks had damped the red clay of which the track was composed, making an ideal surface for the impression of tracks. In this damp clay I had left tracks and over my tracks I now found the splayed out pug marks of the tigress, where she had jumped down from the rocks, gone along the track for a few yards, and then entered the brushwood where I had seen the movement. The tigress was probably familiar with every foot of the ground and having been given no opportunity of killing me at the rocks, was now taking a short cut to the second hairpin with the object of intercepting me. The karker had unwittingly saved me from what might have been a very unpleasant experience and at the same time had deprived the old tigress of relating to her next batch of cubs, how cleverly she had outwitted a gunman.

Further progress along the track was now unsafe, so I followed the karker up the glade, and turning to the left worked my way down, over open ground, to the road below. Had there been sufficient day-light I believe I could that evening, have turned the tables on the tigress, for the conditions, after she left the rocks, were all in my favour.

I have made mention elsewhere of the sense that warns one of impending danger and will not labour the subject further, beyond stating that this sense is a very real one and that I do not know, nor can I explain, what brings it into operation. On this occasion I had neither heard nor seen the tigress, nor had I received any indication from bird or beast of her presence, and yet I knew, without any shadow of a doubt, that she was sheltering among the rocks, and that because of this knowledge I was able to pass the danger point without mishap.

To those of my readers who have had the patience to accompany me so far in my narrative, I would like to give a detailed account of my next and final meeting with the tigress.

The meeting took place on the 11th April 1930, nineteen days after my arrival at Kala Agar.

I had gone out that day at 2 p.m. along the forest road to tie up my three buffaloes, when at a point a mile from the bungalow where the road crosses a ridge and goes from the North to the West face of the Kala Agar range, I came on a party of men who had been out collecting firewood. In the party was an old man who, pointing down the hill to a thicket of young oak trees some five hundred yards from the road, said it was in that thicket the man-eater, a month previously, had killed his son, a lad of 18 years of age. At the spot where we were standing, a foot path took off, going down the hill to the valley below, and zigzagging up the opposite pine clad slope, to rejoin the road, two miles further on. The path passed close to the thicket indicated by the old man, and to humour him, I said I would go down and tie up a buffalo near the thicket. Handing the other two buffaloes over to the party of men to take back to the bungalow, I walked down the path, accompanied by two of my own men, and followed by the remaining buffalo.

Close to the oak thicket I found an open patch of ground, with a pine sapling growing on it. Cutting down the sapling I tied the buffalo to the stump, and while one of the men was cutting grass for the buffalo, I made the other man climb up an oak tree, instructing him to keep tapping the trunk with the back of his axe, and at the same time calling as loudly as he could, in the manner common to our hill folk, when out grazing cattle. While the two men were so engaged I took up a position on a rock at the outer edge of the clearing from where the hill dropped steeply down to the valley below.

The man on the ground had made several trips with the grass he had cut, and the man on the tree was alternately shouting and singing lustily, while I stood on the rock smoking, with the rifle in the hollow of my left arm when, all at once, I became aware that the man-eater had arrived. Beckoning to the man on the ground to come to the rock, I whistled to attract the attention of the man on the tree and signalled to him to remain quiet. The ground on three sides was comparatively open. The man on the tree was to my left front, the man on the ground had been in front of me while the buffalo was on my right. In this area the tigress could not have approached without my having seen her; and as she *had* approached, there was only one place where she could now be; and that was behind, and immediately below me. When I had climbed the rock to take up my position I had noticed that the outer face was smooth and slightly overhanging, and though it would have been possible for the tigress to climb the rock it was very unlikely she would attempt to do so. About eight feet of the rock was visible and below that the rock was masked by thick undergrowth and young saplings. I have no doubt that the tigress, attracted as I had intended she should be, by the noise my man was making, had from a distance seen me, and that it was while she was in the bushes at the foot of the rock looking for a way up, that I had become aware of her presence. My change of front, coupled with the silence of the man on the tree, may have had the effect of making her suspicious; any way, after a lapse of a few minutes I heard a twig snap a little way down the hill side; thereafter the tension relaxed. An opportunity lost; but there was still a very good chance of getting a shot, for she would undoubtedly return before long, and when she found us gone would probably content herself with killing the buffalo. There were still four or five hours of daylight, and by crossing the valley and going up the opposite slope I would be able to overlook the whole of the hill side on which the buffalo was tethered. The shot, if I did get one, would have to be a long one from two to three hundred yards, and even if I only wounded her I would have a blood trail to follow, which would be better than feeling about for her in hundreds of square miles of jungle, as I had been doing these many months.

The men were a difficulty. To have sent them back alone would have been nothing short of murder, so of necessity I kept them with me.

Tying the buffalo in such a manner as to make it impossible for the tigress to carry it off, I left the open ground and rejoined the path to carry out the plan I have outlined.

Proceeding about a hundred yards along the path, I came to a ravine, which the path crossed. On the far side of the ravine the path entered very heavy undergrowth, and as it was inadvisable to go into thick jungle with two men following me, I decided to take to the ravine, follow it to its junction with the valley, and work up the valley and back on to the path.

The ravine was four or five feet deep, and as I stepped down into it a nightjar fluttered off a rock, on which I had put my hand. On looking at the spot from which the bird had risen I saw two eggs. These eggs, straw coloured, with rich brown markings, were of a most unusual shape, one being long and very pointed, while the other was as round as a marble, and as my collection lacked nightjar eggs I decided to add this odd clutch to it. I had no receptacle of any kind in which to carry these eggs, so cupping my left hand I placed the eggs in it and packed them round with a little moss.

As I went along the ravine the banks became higher, and sixty yards from where I had entered it I came on a deep drop of some twelve to fourteen feet. The water that rushes down all these hill ravines in the rains had worn the rock as smooth as glass, and as it was too steep to offer a foot hold, I handed the rifle to the men and, sitting on the edge, proceeded to slide down. My feet had hardly touched the sandy bottom when the two men with a flying leap landed, one on either side of me and thrusting the rifle into my hand asked in a very agitated manner if I had heard the tiger. On my questioning them as to what kind of noise they had heard, they said it was a low deep-throated growl, from somewhere close at hand, but exactly from which direction the sound had come, they were unable to say.

Where we stood we had the smooth steep rock behind us, to our right a wall of rock slightly leaning over the ravine and fifteen feet high, and a bank of tumbled rocks thirty or forty feet high on our left. The sandy bed of the ravine was roughly forty feet long by ten wide. At the lower end of this sandy patch a great pine tree had fallen across the ravine, damming it up and the collection of sand was due to this dam. The wall of overhanging rock came to an end twelve or fifteen feet from the fallen tree, and as I approached the end, my feet making no sound on the sand, I saw that the sandy bed continued round to the back of the rock, which I can best describe as a slab of slate two feet thick, standing up not quite perpendicularly on one of its long sides. As I cleared the rock I looked back over my right shoulder – and looked straight into the tigress's eyes.

I would like you, my readers, to appreciate the position.

The sandy bed behind the rock was quite flat. To the right of it was the smooth slate of rock fifteen feet high and leaning slightly outwards, to the left was a scoured out steep bank also some fifteen feet high and overhung by a tangle of thorn bushes, while at the far end was a slide similar to, but a little higher than, the one I had glissaded down. The sandy bed, enclosed by these three natural walls, was about twenty feet long and half as wide, and lying on it, with her fore paws stretched out and her hind legs well tucked under her, was the tigress. Her head which was raised a few inches off her paws was eight feet from me, and on her face was a smile similar to that one sees on the face of a dog, welcoming his master after a long absence.

Two thoughts flashed through my mind, one, that it was up to me to make the next move, and the other, that the move must be made in such a way as not to alarm the tigress.

The rifle was in my right hand held diagonally across my chest, with the safety catch off, and in order to get it to bear on the tigress the muzzle would have to be swung round half a circle.

The movement of swinging round the muzzle with one hand was started very slowly, and when a quarter of a circle had been made, the stock came in contact with my right side. It was now necessary to extend my arm, and as the stock cleared my side, the swing was continued. My arm was now at full stretch and the weight of the rifle, which was fortunately a .275 was beginning to tell. There was now only a little further for the muzzle to go, and the tigress was still looking up at me with the expression still on her face.

How long it took for the rifle to make the half circle I am not in a position to say. To me, looking into the tigress's eyes and unable therefore to follow the movements of the barrel it appeared that my arm was paralysed, and that the swing would never be completed. However the movement was completed at last, and as soon as the rifle was pointing at the tigress's body, I pressed the trigger.

I heard the report, exaggerated in that restricted space, and I felt the jar of the recoil, and but for these tangible proofs that the rifle had gone off, I might, for all the immediate result the shot produced, have been in the grip of one of those awful nightmares, where motion is arrested at the critical moment.

For a perceptible fraction of time the tigress remained perfectly still and then, very slowly, her head sank onto her outstretched paws, while at the same time a jet of blood issued from the bullet hole (the bullet had shattered the upper portion of her heart).

The men now came forward to relieve me of the empty rifle and to see what I had fired at, and as my legs very suddenly seemed to be in need of a rest, I made for the fallen pine, and sat down. Even before looking at her pads I knew it was the Chowgarh tigress I had sent to the happy hunting grounds, and that the shears that had assisted her to cut the threads of sixty-four human lives – the people of the district put the number at twice that figure – had, while the game was in her hands, turned, and cut the thread of her own life.

While the two men went up the hill to free the buffalo and secure the rope that was required for our further operations, I went up the ravine to restore the eggs to their rightful owner. I plead guilty of being superstitious. For three long periods, extending over a whole year, I had tried to get a shot at the tigress, and had failed, and now within a few minutes of having picked up the eggs my luck had changed. And not only had the eggs brought me luck in enabling me to kill the tigress, but I am also convinced they saved my life: for had I had both hands on the rifle when I stepped clear of the rock, I should instinctively have swung round to face the tigress, and the spring that was arrested by my lack of movement, would inevitably have been launched.

The eggs which all this time had remained in the hollow of my left hand were still warm when I replaced them in the little depression in the rock that did duty as a nest, and when I passed that way half an hour later, the eggs had vanished under the brooding mother whose colouring so exactly matched the mottled rock, that it was difficult for me, who knew the position, to distinguish her from her surroundings.

The buffalo, who after months of care, was now so tame that it followed like a dog, came scrambling down the hill in the wake of the men, nosed the tigress and lay down on the sand to chew the cud of contentment, while we lashed the tigress to the dry sapling the men had cut.

I had tried to get the men to return to the bungalow for help, but this they would not hear of doing. With no one would they share the honour of carrying in the man-eater, and if I would lend a hand, the task, with frequent halts for rest, would not be difficult. We were three hefty men – two accustomed from childhood to carrying heavy loads – and all three hardened by a life of exposure; but even so, the task we had set ourselves was a superhuman one.

The path was too narrow and too winding for the pole to which the tigress was lashed, so we had to go straight up the hill which was overgrown with raspberry and briar bushes, on the thorns of which we left most of our clothing and an amount of skin which made bathing for many days a painful operation.

It was on the 11th of April, 1930, that we carried the tigress to the Kala Agar Forest Bungalow; and from that date to this, no human being has been killed over the 1500 square miles of mountain and valley over which the Chowgarh tigress, for a period of five years, held sway.*

*In the original work, Corbett sometimes spells "Dalkania" this way, and at other times "Dalkanyia". We have consistently retained the former spelling.

4

A Half-Brother's Tale

Extracts from Charles Doyle's *The Taming of the Jungle*

Jim Corbett self-published his first book, *Jungle Stories*, in 1935, at the age of sixty. He then reworked these stories, along with several others, into *Man-Eaters of Kumaon*, which appeared nine years later in 1944, when he was sixty-nine. The tales of adventure in his books describe experiences that had occurred at least twenty years in the past. At first, Corbett seems to have been a reluctant writer, though once he found his stride he produced his six books at a hectic pace, especially for an elderly man who suffered from many infirmities, including the chronic after effects of "tick typhus" and malaria.

But a little-known fact, which his sister Maggie recalls, is that there was another writer in the family, their eldest half-brother, Charles Doyle. Having grown up in Nainital and Kaladhungi with his mother, stepfather, and younger brothers and sisters, Charles was sent to Edinburgh, where he completed a medical degree. After opening a private practice in Scotland, he then emigrated to the United States and ended up working as a doctor in Santa Cruz, California. It's not clear whether he ever visited India again, though it seems unlikely.

Nevertheless, Charles Doyle was deeply influenced by his early years in Nainital and the family's winter home at Kaladhungi. He was more than twenty years older than Jim (their mother married her first husband at the age of fourteen, according to Maggie's recollections). In addition to being a physician, Charles Doyle had literary ambitions and published several collections of verse as well as a novel, *The Taming of the Jungle*, which was published in 1899 by J.B. Lippincott in the United States. When it came out, Jim would have been twenty-four – around the time he was working as a railway contractor at Mokameh Ghat and before he began hunting man-eaters. Charles Doyle would undoubtedly have sent copies of the book home to his mother, and the family must have read his novel with interest and amusement, as well as some consternation!

Doyle had a fertile and romantic imagination. He aspired to the airy, overblown prose of Rudyard Kipling's least successful stories and seemed to believe that fiction gave him a licence to combine his nostalgia for the Terai with a fecund sense of melodrama. Living close to Hollywood, he took to heart American cinema's passion for suspending disbelief. In essence, he was a terrible writer.

Doyle's book is set in the same territory as many of Jim Corbett's stories, namely the foothills and thickly forested lowlands near Kaladhungi and Haldwani. It contains brave white hunters, one of whom is named "Charlie Sahib", as well as forest dwellers and bullock-cart drivers. There are man-eaters too! The female character, Chambeli, obviously personifies Doyle's sense of romance and the seductive allure of the jungle.

In many ways this book is the antithesis of Jim Corbett's writing, which is precise, understated, and with an authentic sense of place as well as a taut narrative structure. One can only imagine the young Corbett reading Charles Doyle's *The Taming of the Jungle* and shaking his head in dismay at the absurd portrait it presents of the people and forests of India. Many years later, when Jim picked up a pen himself, it is very likely that he consciously resolved to write books that were nothing like the unconvincing tales his half-brother had published.

The Taming of the Jungle

By Dr. C.W. Doyle

Philadelphia & London
J.B. Lippincott Company
1899

*Extracts**

CHAPTER XI

The Lame Tiger of Huldwani

It was in the middle of May – just before the beginning of the lesser rains – that Ram Deen and certain wayfarers sat round a handful of fire at Lal Kooah from mere force of habit, for the heat of the evening was great, and not a breath of air stirred in the jungle. The sâl trees had lost their leaves and looked like ghosts; the grass had been burnt in all directions; and as the sun set in the copper sky, it lit up a landscape that might have stood for the ""abomination of desolation."

The dry chirping of the crickets, just beginning to tune their first uneasy strains, accorded with the unholy scene. Even the horses waiting for the mail-cart were imbued with the depressing influence of the season, and hung their heads with a sense of despair, as though they thought the blessed monsoon would never set in.

No one spoke, and the hookah passed from hand to hand in a dreary silence. Suddenly, the attention of those assembled was attracted by the curious action of a bya (tailor) bird in a

*No attempt has been made to untangle the eccentricities of Doyle's spelling, vocabulary, and usage. And for our purposes, Doyle's sequence has been slightly rearranged by repositioning his Chapter X.

neighboring mimosa tree. It was calling frantically, and dropping lower from bough to bough, as though against its will.

"Nâg!" exclaimed the bunnia; and, directed by his remark, all eyes were turned to the foot of the tree, where an enormous cobra with expanded hood was swaying its head from side to side, and drawing the wretched bird to its doom through the fascination of fear.

Ram Deen, whose sympathies were always with the weak and defenceless, rose to his feet, and, throwing a dry clod of earth at the reptile, drove the creature from the tree; whilst the bird, released from its hypnotic influence, flew away.

"Brothers," said Ram Deen, "fear is the father of all sins, and the cause of most calamities. He who feareth not death is a king in his own right, and dieth but once; but a coward – shabash! who can count his pangs?"

"Ho! ho!" chuckled the little bullock driver; "Ram Deen, The Fearless, shall live to be an hundred years old."

"Nay, Goor Dutt," said Ram Deen, gravely regarding the little man, "I, too, have known fear. No man may drive the mail to Kaladoongie without looking on death."

Ram Deen smoked awhile in silence; and, when the expectation of his listeners was wrought to a proper pitch, he went on: "Ye all knew Nandha, the hostler, who used to go with me last year from this stage to Kaladoongie?"

"Ay, coach-wan ji," responded the carrier for the others. "'Tis a great telling, but not known to these honorable wayfarers who come from beyond Moradabad."

"Brothers, ye saw the plight of the bya bird but now; so was it with Nandha," said Ram Deen.

"One evening, ere the mail arrived, he called me to where he stood by the kikar tree yonder, looking down at the ground. In the dust of the road were large footprints."

"'These be the spoor of a tiger lame in its left hind foot,' I said to Nandha; 'see, here it crouched on its belly, and wiped away the wheel tracks made by the mail-cart this morning.'

"''Tis the lame tiger of Huldwani, coach-wan; he is old, and he hunteth man. Gunga said he is hunting elsewhere tonight!' replied Nandha.

"When we came within a mile of the Bore bridge that night, the horses stopped suddenly; they were wild with fear, and refused to move. The night was as dark as the inside of a gourd, and beyond the circle of light made by our lanterns we could discern in the middle of the road two balls of fire close to the ground.

"'Bâg! (tiger),' said Nandha, as he climbed over into the back seat; 'we be dead men, Ram Deen.'

"'Blow!' I commanded, giving him the bugle; and as he startled the jungle with a blast, I gathered up the reins, and, adding my voice to the terrors of Nandha's music, I urged the horses with whip and yell to fury of speed; and the light of the lanterns showed the great beast leaping into the darkness to escape our onset.

"Nandha ceased not from blowing on the bugle till I took it from him by force at the door of the post-office at Kaladoongie.

"They gave him bhang to smoke and arrack to drink ere he slept that night, for his great fear had deprived him of reason for awhile; and he looked round him as though he expected to see the tiger's eyes everywhere.

"'The bâg followed me to the hither side of the Bore bridge,' he said to me next morning, as we prepared to return to Lal Kooah. But I laughed at his fears, to give him courage.

"'It is a devil,' he whispered, looking cautiously round him, and I saw that the light of his reason flickered.

"When we came to the Bore bridge, Nandha leaped to the ground, and in the dim light of the morning I could see the tracks of a great beast on the ground, to which he pointed; and, even as we looked, there came the roar of a tiger. I could scarce hold the horses whilst Nandha, whose limbs were stiff with fear, scrambled into the back seat of the mail-cart.

"When a tiger puts its mouth to the ground and gives voice, no man may tell whence the sound comes; so I stayed not to see, if I might, where the danger lay, but gave the horses free rein.

"As we cleared the end of the bridge, Nandha screamed, 'Bâg, bâg!' and glancing back, I saw the tiger in full pursuit of us, and within a hundred paces.

"'Blow!' I commanded, handing the bugle to Nandha; but, though he took it from me, he appeared not to understand what he was required to do.

"'Blow!' said I, once more, shaking him; but he took no heed of me, and was as a man who walks in his sleep. So I put my arm round him and lifted him on to the front seat beside me; and even as I pulled him to me, his head was drawn over his shoulder by the spell of fear. There was a foam on his lips and on his beard, and he shook so that I feared he would fall off the mail-cart.

"'Be brave, Nandha,' I shouted to him, 'the beast is lame, and we shall soon leave it behind.' For answer, he turned his face to me for one instant, and his lips framed the word 'bâg', but no sound came therefrom.

"Suddenly, he laughed like a child that is pleased with a toy, babbling, and saying, 'How beautiful is my lord! Soft be the road to his feet! But, look! my lord limpeth; belike he hath a thorn in his foot.' As he rose, I put an arm round him and forced him down again; and at that instant the tiger uttered another roar. The horses swerved, and would have left the road in their fear, had I not put forth the full strength of both my arms; and as soon as Nandha felt himself free, he leaped to the ground, and advanced towards the tiger. He walked joyously, as a loyal servant who goeth to meet his lord.

"Looking over my shoulder (for now the horses were in the middle of the road, which here stretched straight ahead of us), I beheld Nandha proceed towards the tiger, which now crouched in the road, waiting for him, its tail waving from side to side. When he was within five paces of the beast, he salaamed to the ground, and as he stooped the tiger sprang on him with another roar, and throwing him over its shoulder it bounded with him into the jungle.

"More there is to tell concerning the lame tiger of Huldwani, but here is the mail-cart, and here is that which had saved Nandha's life had I not also looked upon fear that morning."

Putting the bugle to his mouth, Ram Deen blew a blast that would have routed any jungle creature within hearing, and which made the leaves of the peepul tree overhead rattle as he dashed away on the mail-cart.

CHAPTER XII

How Nandha was Avenged

The travellers from beyond Moradabad having reached Kaladoongie, were discovered to be men of consequence by the Thanadar, and were invited by him to join the circle of the great round his fire on the evening of their arrival.

It was very warm, and the dismal silence was only accented by the distant howl of a lonely jackal. The sheet lightning flickered fitfully over the foothills, mocking the gasping Terai with its faint promise of a coming change.

The conversation round the fire flagged, and the hookah passed languidly from hand to hand. Those present would have retired to sleep, had sleep been possible; but as that was a consummation not easily attained at this season of the year, they preferred their present miseries to those that come in the wakeful night watches when the Terai is athirst.

Ram Deen's arrival was a nightly boon to those who were wont to assemble round the Thanadar's fire; there was always the possibility of his having news; and, besides, men seemed to acquire fresh vitality from contact with his vigorous personality.

The strangers were especially grateful for his arrival; and when he had taken his usual place beside the fire, the hookah was at once passed to him.

"Any tidings, coach-wan ji?" inquired the Thanadar.

"None, sahib; save that the great frog in the well at Lal Kooah – who is as old as the well, and wiser than most men – gave voice just ere I started, and the bunnia said it was a sure sign of rain within two days, as the frog's warning had never been known to fail."

"Nana Debi said it be so," exclaimed the little carrier, "for my bullocks be starved for the lack of green food, and bhoosa (chaff) is past my means."

"Thou shouldst not complain, Goor Dutt," said Ram Deen, with a smile; "their very leanness is thy passport through the jungle. Fatter kine had been devoured, and their driver with them, long ere this."

Hint of danger that might be encountered in the jungle having been thus given, one of the strangers was moved to ask concerning the lame tiger of Huldwani, part of whose biography they had heard from Ram Deen at Lal Kooah on the previous day.

"Coach-wan ji, wast thou not afraid to carry the mail after the slaying of thy hostler, Nandha?"

"Those who carry the Queen's mail may not stop for fear. Nevertheless, fear rode with me a day and a night after the death of Nandha."

"It is a great telling," said the little carrier, nodding at the wayfarers, whilst Ram Deen "drank tobacco."

When Ram Deen had passed the hookah to his neighbor, he went on:

"Brothers, on the day that Nandha was carried off by the tiger, I sent word to the postmaster of Naini Tal concerning the killing, and the out-going mail brought me word that the sircar (government) would send me help.

"Ye know that a tiger kills not two days in succession; so I had no fear when I traversed the road to and from Lal Kooah till the second day after the slaying of Nandha. Ere I started on that morning, the munshi told me to drive to the dâk-bungalow for a sahib who had been sent to slay the slayer of men.

"Brothers, when I went to the dâk-bungalow, there came forth to me a man-child – a Faringi – whose chin was as smooth as the palm of my hand.

"I would have laughed, but that I thought of the tiger that, I knew, would be waiting for us; and taking pity on him, I said, 'The jungle hereabout is full of wild fowl, sahib, an 'twere pity, when shikar is so plentiful, you should waste the morning looking for a budmash tiger who will not come forth for two days as yet.'

"He answered me never a word, but went into the dâk-bungalow for something he had forgotten; and, whilst he was gone, his butler spake to me, saying, 'Coach-wan, make no mistake; thy life depends upon thy doing the sahib's bidding. He is a very Rustum, and he knoweth not fear, for all he is so young.'

"'He is a man after my own heart then, sirdar; but, mashallah! I would he had a beard,' I replied.

"Presently the young sahib came forth with an empty bottle in one hand and his gun in the other. Throwing the bottle into the air, he shattered it with a bullet ere it reached the ground. Startled by the report, a jackal fled from the rear of the cook-house towards the jungle, and the sahib stopped its flight with another bullet. Then, replenishing his gun, he took his seat beside me on the mail-cart, saying 'Blow on thy bugle, coach-wan, and announce our coming to Shere Bahadoor, His Majesty the Tiger.'

"It was a brave jawan (youth), brothers; but he was very young, and, belike, he had a mother; so I swore in my beard to save him, whatever might befall.

"As we proceeded, he questioned me concerning the killing of Nandha, speaking lightly, as one who goeth to shoot black partridge.

"'He is lame, coach-wan, and will doubtless be waiting for us by the Bore bridge,' said the sahib. 'As soon as he appears, stay the horses for an instant whilst I get off the mail-cart, and then return when your horses will let you.'

"'Bethink thee, sahib,' I answered; 'the Lame One of Huldwani is old and cunning; it is no fawn thou seekest this morning. Perchance the sircar will dispatch some great shikari to help thee in this hunting. Gunga said we may not meet the tiger; but if we should, shame befall me if I permit thee to leave the mail-cart whilst the horses are able to run!'

"For answer, my brothers, the sahib flushed red, and, calling me coward, he drave his elbow into my stomach with such force that the reins fell from my hands. Taking them up, the while I fought for my breath, he turned the horses round, saying, 'A jackal may not hunt a tiger! I have need of a man with me this morning, and Goor Deen, my butler, shall take thy place.'

"'The sahib, being a man, will not blacken my face in the eyes of Kaladoongie,' I said. 'I spake for thy sake, sahib; but I will drive thee to Jehandum an' thou wilt, – for no man hath ever called me coward before.'

"Then the sahib looked in my face, as I tucked the ends of my beard under my puggri; and seeing that my eyes met his four-square, he gave up the reins to me, saying, 'If thou playest me false I will kill thee like a dog;' and he showed me the hilt of a pistol that he had in his pocket.

"We spake no more together, but when we came to the Bore bridge I shook the jungle with a blast from my bugle.

"'Shabash! coach-wan,' exclaimed the sahib; 'thou art a man, indeed, and shalt have Shere Bahadoor's skin as recompense for the hurt to thy stomach. Bid him come again.'

"Half a mile beyond the bridge, as we sped along the level road above the river, I again blew upon the bugle. The sound had scarcely ceased, when we heard the angry roar of a charging tiger.

"'Stop!' exclaimed the sahib; and I threw the frightened horses on their haunches, whilst he leaped to the ground.

"Then, whilst the horses flew along the road, I looked back over my shoulder and beheld the Lame One bound into the middle of the road; and the sahib blew on his fingers, as one would whistle to a dog. The great beast stopped on the instant and crouched on the ground, ready to spring on the sahib as he advanced towards it, and I prayed to Nana Debi to befriend the young fool.

"When he was within thirty paces or so from the tiger, the sahib halted and brought the gun to his shoulder. The next instant there was the crack of a rifle, and the Lame One leaped straight into the air.

"I knew the tiger was dead; and immediately thereafter the mail-cart ran into a bank and spilled me on the road. Leaving the stunned horses tied to a tree, I proceeded to seek the sahib.

"Wah ji, wah! brothers, we must pay taxes to the Faringis until we can raise sons like theirs. When I joined the boy sahib he was smoking, and taking the measure of the tiger with a tape!

"His bullet had struck the beast between the eyes, and the Lame One had died at the hands of a man!"

CHAPTER X

Cœlum, Non Animum Mutant

The Commissioner of Kumaon had arrived at Kaladoongie in the course of his winter tour of inspection, and the same evening Joti Prshad, his butler, sat beside the Thanadar on a charpoi and smoked with metropolitan ease amidst the awe-struck notables of the jungle village.

Ram Deen alone was not abashed, and puffed his hookah unconcernedly, although Joti Prshad told many wonderful things of the sahiblogue, and spoke concerning the doings of the great world of Naini Tal during the greater rains.

Joti Prshad was a small man, and Ram Deen's *blasé* mood galled his sense of superiority; it was but right that he should snub this exasperatingly cool villager.

"Thanadar ji," he began, "thou and I know that nowhere in Hindoostan is there such greatness assembled as at Naini Tal during the Greater Barsât."

"Men say that the governor-general still goeth to Simla, but, doubtless, the sirdar knoweth best," said Ram Deen.

"The Lât-sahib, indeed, goeth to Simla, but those with him be mere karanis (clerks), and shopkeepers, and half-castes. 'Tis plain thou hast not seen Naini Tal, coach-wan."

"The Terai sufficeth me, Joti Prshad."

"They say," piped Goor Dutt, the little bullock driver, "that the mem-sahibs at Naini Tal bare their shoulders and bosoms and dance with strange men. Toba, toba!"

This being an indisputable fact, and one to which Joti Prshad had never reconciled himself, the latter did not speak, and the diversion thus made by the byl-wan was felt by all to be in Ram Deen's favor.

Taking advantage of the silence of Joti Prshad, Ram Deen went on: "The people of Naini Tal come and go, but the children of the Terai never forget their mother. What sayest thou, Thanadar ji?"

"'Tis even so, brothers," said the Thanadar, with the gravity of one who is in authority and under the stress of weighing his words.

As they evidently waited for him to proceed, the Thanadar continued: "The jungle is our father and our mother, and the huldoo trees our near kin, O my brothers; and we who have once seen the beauty of the morning in the jungle, and the rye-fields laughing in the clearings in the winter, may not live elsewhere."

"Ay, Thanadar ji," said Ram Deen; "and, moreover, the senses of those who live in bazaars are asleep as with bhang, and they cannot see nor hear the wonders of God."

A general "humph" of assent followed Ram Deen's speech.

"If the sirdar will stay with us we will show him whereof we speak," said the Thanadar. But the butler had fond recollections of Oude and the rose-fields of Shahjahanpoor, where they make attar, and shook his head dissentingly. So the Thanadar went on: "Many seasons since, a holy man – a Sunyasi – who had given up his wife and children and lived in a hollow tree by the Rock of Khalsi (whereon are written the laws of the great king Asoka) returned to Gurruckpoor, his native village, when he felt the Great Darkness coming on. He told the village Brahmin that he longed for death, but that he could not die outside of the Terai."

After a pause, during which the bubbling of his narghili was heard, the Thanadar said: "It is the same with all who are born in the Terai, – Faringi and Padhani, Brahmin and Dome, Sunyasi and fair woman, – all are alike in bondage, and return, sooner or later, to their jungle mother. Listen. Twelve years ago there came to Gurruckpoor to hunt big game an Englishman named Fisher Sahib. He was of those favored by God who have much wealth, and to whom sport standeth for occupation. As he was accustomed to fulfil his heart's desires, he hired two shooting elephants from the Rajah of Rampore, – one for himself and the other for his mem-sahib, who accompanied him. And he had a great camp, and many servants, and beaters, and shikaris, chief of whom was Juggoo, whose fame as a hunter reached from Phillibeet to Dehra. He it was who always rode with the sahib in his howdah, and he had command from the mem-sahib never to leave the sahib's side in the jungle, in that he was rash and loved danger, and many a time fell into it unawares by reason that he saw not clearly except he looked through a piece of glass that he wore in one eye.

"One day the sahib had shot a deer, and let himself down from his elephant – Juggoo going with him – to give it hallal, according to the rule of the Koran, – for he intended the deer as a gift to the Mussulmanis in his camp. As he bent over the deer to cut its throat with his khookri, a great boar ran upon them from a thicket. Juggoo uttered a cry of warning, but ere the sahib could find his sight the boar was upon them, and Juggoo thrust himself in its way and got his death, or the sahib had been killed.

"So they carried the dead man to the camp, where his daughter, Chambeli, having cooked his evening meal, awaited the return of her father. She was fifteen years in age, and a widow, – for her betrothed husband and all his people had died five years before of The Sickness (small-pox); so she had returned to her father, and had cared for his house ever since. And Kali Dass, who was learning jungle-craft from her father, would have had her to mistress. 'Come and live with me, my beloved, beyond the head-waters of the Bore Nuddee,' he had pleaded; 'and when thy hair hath grown again none shall know thou art a widow, and the people of the foothills shall wonder at thy beauty.'

"'But I shall know and Nana Debi, – and the others matter not, Kali Dass,'" she replied firmly.

"So Kali Dass went his way; and the young man and Chambeli looked at each other, but spake no more together.

"The mem-sahib it was who told Chambeli of her father's death, Kali Dass standing by, and she turned on him like a leopard bereft of its young and upbraided him, saying, 'Hadst thou been a man, Kali Dass, my father were still living.' Thereafter she swooned, and the mem-sahib laid her on her own couch, and held her in her arms and comforted her, because Juggoo had died to save the sahib.

"Then for that she was childless and very wealthy, and could do whatsoever seemed good in her eyes, the mem-sahib took Chambeli across the Black Water. They brought her up as their own kin, teaching her whatsoever it is fitting the daughter of a Faringi should know, and training her to work amongst our women and children when they should be afflicted with sickness; and, furthermore, she was to turn them from Nana Debi to the God of the Faringis.

"Moreover, to aid her in her work she was married to a young English padre; and they came to Kaladoongie six years ago, when the next new-year festival of the Faringis shall arrive. And because we knew her and still remembered Juggoo, her father, we of Kaladoongie waited on her at the dâk-bungalow on the day she returned.

"She came out to us on the veranda, dressed in the garments of a mem-sahib, and we saw that she was a woman grown and in the mid-noon of her beauty. She was glad to see us, calling us all by our names, and we greeted her with such gifts as we could, – fruit and flowers and sweetmeats. Last of all came Kali Dass, and behind him four men bearing a leopard but newly slain, slung from a pole.

"They laid the beast at her feet, and Chambeli laughed and clapped her hands till the little padre, her husband, frowned at her; whereon her nostrils twitched and she looked at him in wonderment, as though she saw for the first time that he was a small man with a pale face, and void of authority.

"Then turning to Kali Dass she said in our Terai tongue, 'Is it well with thee, shikari ji? Thou art doubtless married and happy?'

"And he said, 'Nay; I have no spouse, save only my junglecraft.'

"'And the jungle?' she asked, looking on the ground.

"'It is my father and my mother, and fairer than any of its daughters, mem-sahib. But thou hast been in great cities, and across the Black Water; thou hast read in books, and hast changed thy gods, – what shouldst thou care for the jungle?'

"'It is the garden of God, Kali Dass, and I am fain to see it again, for I am a Padhani born, and a daughter of the Terai.'

"Ere she gave us leave to depart it was arranged that she and the padre sahib, accompanied by me and Kali Dass, should start in the early morning and follow the Bore Nuddee backward into the foothills.

"Kali Dass was at the dâk-bungalow before me in the morning; and he was dressed in holiday clothes; his face shone, and behind one ear he had placed a marigold.

"When the padre and his mem-sahib came forth from their chamber, behold! she was dressed as a Padhani; and she was the Chambeli we knew of old, only taller.

"'I am but a Padhani,' she explained, 'and shall get nearer to my people the more I am like to them.'

"It was a time of great stillness when we started, for the morning was just born, and the dew lay on all things. Taking the road to Naini Tal, we struck into the jungle when we came to the path that leads to the ford of the Bore Nuddee, and Chambeli alighted from her pony and walked in front of the rest with Kali Dass. A faint flush showed in the east, and presently a jungle-cock greeted the dawn. Chambeli stopped, and, with joy in her face, she turned round to the padre sahib, exclaiming, 'Didst hear that?' And he laughed, saying, 'It was but the crowing of a cock.'

"'But it came out of the stillness of the morning, and the dew accorded with it, – and it was a wild thing, – but how shouldst thou understand? thou art not of the Terai,' she said.

"Soon the glow in the east became brighter, and the jungle burst into its morning song. Chambeli stopped and put her hands to her forehead, as if she would remember something; then she said to the shikari, 'Something is lacking, Kali Dass; what is it?' And even as she spake there came the call of a black partridge from a thicket near by: 'Sobhan teri koodruth!' Brothers, ye know that the black partridge is the priest of the Terai, and at its voice Chambeli fled with a cry of joy from the path and into the thick jungle.

"The little padre sahib, knowing not what to think, urged us to follow her. When we came up with her, Kali Dass stood by regarding her with a smile, whilst she lay on the ground with her face buried in the dewy grass, moaning and saying, 'O Jungle Mother, I will never leave thee again, I will never leave thee again!' And the little padre chid her in his own tongue; whereat she rose shuddering; and brushing the dew and the tears from her face, she returned to the path.

"She had eyes and ears for everything that morning, and was as a wild thing that had just fled from captivity.

"When we came to the brow of the hill that slopes down to the ford, the sun rose over the tops of the trees and laid a gleaming sword across the stream; and as we looked at the brightness and wonder of it all there came to us the song of a string of Padhani women approaching the ford. In an instant Chambeli took up the song, and set off swiftly down the narrow path, we following as we could.

"As she neared the ford she lifted her sari and took the water with her bare limbs; and I looked at the little padre, who seemed sore amazed.

"When we had all crossed the ford, Chambeli and Kali Dass were not to be seen on the road that ran by the stream. A traveller on his way to Kaladoongie said he had not met them, and as we questioned him there came the report of a gun.

"'Kali Dass hath met game, padre sahib,' said I.

"'Find them, and bring them back instantly, Thanadar,' commanded the holy man, and his voice shook with anger. "Following the direction of the shot, I came upon their tracks, and thereafter I found a handful of fresh feathers. A few paces beyond lay a small book; it was the sacred book of the Faringis printed in Nagari, and on the first leaf, which was held down by a stone, was writing in English. On the path a pace farther were two sticks crossed, and beyond that other two; and I knew it was the warning of Kali Dass, who must not be followed.

"So I returned with the little book to the padre sahib. And when he had read what was written on the first leaf he trembled and clutched at his throat, and I caught him in my arms as he fell from his horse.

"I returned with him to Kaladoongie; but Chambeli and Kali Dass never came back.

"I showed the writing in the book to Tulsi Ram. Speak, pundit, and tell our brothers what it meant."

Tulsi Ram, pleased and proud to give an exhibition of his scholarship, replied, "Brothers, and you, O Joti Prshad, the writing said: 'Like to like: Kali Dass is of my blood, and the great jungle hath claimed her daughter this day.'"

CHAPTER XV

"Ich Liebe Dich"

Early one morning in December, in the year 186–, I left my camp with a pointer at my heels to explore the foothills to the northwest of Nyagong. The region abounded with iron ore, and the mining syndicate I represented instructed me to conduct my prospecting in a way that would not arouse the suspicion of the manager of another company that had already established iron works at Kaladoongie. So it speedily became noised about in that section of the Terai that I was one of the many Englishmen who spend their leave of absence in the jungle for the purposes of sport.

There was a shrewd nip in the air when I started, and the barrels of my gun were so cold that I was glad I had put on a pair of thick gloves.

The jungle was hardly awake when I struck into the path that skirted the Bore Nuddee. Presently, a green parrot "kr-r-r-d" tentatively, as a faint flush appeared in the cloudless east. A wild boar jumped a fence a few hundred yards ahead of me, followed by the sounder, of which he was chief, as they left the fields they had been marauding during the night. A nilghai, with his wicked-looking horns, soon followed, and lumbered noiselessly away. These were the thieves of the Terai, and they were, naturally, hurrying to their coverts before the coming day should be upon them.

Suddenly, the dewy silence was broken by the invocation of a black partridge, – the muezzin of the jungle. "Sobhan teri koodruth!" How solemnly, and with what splendor of utterance and pause this voice of the Terai announces the miracle of the morning! The cry was taken up and passed on with a significance that dwarfed the passing of the fiery torch as told by Scott in "The Lady of the Lake." And immediately thereafter the jungle was singing its many-voiced matin, not the least "notable note" of which was the challenge of the jungle-cock, who is a native of the Terai, and whose vigorous voice is not raucous with the civilised laryngeal affections of the "tame villatic fowl."

And then, in the awakening of the forest, there came – Italian opera! A well-poised soprano voice silenced the jungle choir by a brilliantly executed chromatic scale, as though the singer were trying her voice. Finding it flexible enough for her purpose, she launched into the difficult – and abominable – aria, "Di tale amore che dirsi" in "Il Trovatore." She suddenly stopped, as though she were ashamed of the rubbish she sang; and, after a pause of half a minute, my soul was stirred by the air of Beethoven's immortal "Ich Liebe Dich," sung to the following words, which were beautifully enunciated:

I love thee, dear! All words would fail
To tell the true and tender theme;
Such ardent thoughts, and passion pale,
And humble suit, I fondly deem,
Would need a poet's rapturous mind.

Oh! if fit words could but be bought,
If Love's own speech I could but find,
I'd sell my soul to express my thought,
So you should in Love's toils be caught!

Oh! then a kindlier sun would shine,
The vermeiled flowers would look more fair,
The common world would seem divine,
And daily things appear most rare;
My soul, a soaring lark, would rise
To greet the morning of thy love
So sweetly dawning in thine eyes,
And in thy smiles, which should approve.

The tender charm of the sweet old song – now utterly neglected for more brazen utterances, and which only Beethoven could have written – was thoroughly appreciated by the singer.

Wishing to see her without myself being discovered, and hoping to hear her sing again, I "stalked" her – and, behold, she was a Padhani! I couldn't be mistaken, for she was singing David's "O ma maitresse," as I watched her from behind the bole of a great huldoo tree.

A little boy, about three years in age, played beside her as she sat on a fallen tree trunk and took part in the matin of the Terai. There was a noble breadth between her eyes that reminded one of the Sistine Madonna, and an air of repose about her figure which was set off by her simple garments.

She was, without doubt, Chambeli, the Padhani protégé of the Fishers, whose flight from her husband, the Rev. John

Trusler, immediately after her return to the Terai, had been the sensation of the season at Naini Tal a few years ago.

Snapping a dry twig with my foot to attract her attention, I stepped into the open and approached her. Her first impulse was to flee, but she quickly regained her composure and awaited me, standing, her eyes meeting mine without the least embarrassment.

"Your singing attracted me," I began, taking off my hat to her.

"Yes?" she replied, evidently not at all anxious to come to my relief in the awkward position I had sought.

"It was very beautiful – "

"And it is finished," she interrupted. There was a slight tone of contempt in her voice as she thus gave me to understand that my presence was unwelcome. But, as a student of psychology, I was not to be so easily moved from my design of "investigating the case" before me.

"The Rev. John Trusler is dead." I paused awhile to see how she would be affected. Then, as she gave no sign of emotion, I went on, "He hanged himself a few days after you left him."

"My God!" she exclaimed, putting her hand to her side and seating herself on the fallen tree.

The child, who had been clinging to his mother's dress and regarding me with round, brown eyes, began to cry when he saw his mother's sudden emotion. She took him up in her arms and cuddled his head to her bosom, saying in the Padhani patois, "Mea mithoo, mea mithoo! hush, my butcha."

In the silence that ensued after the child had been quieted there came the regular stroke of a woodman's axe, and presently the refrain of a Padhani song sung by a man.

When the woman had regained her calm, she looked up at me somewhat defiantly and said, "What business had they to come between me and my jungle mother? What right had they to impose moral shackles on one who was above their petty codes?"

"The Fishers were moved by kindness, surely; they educated you, and Christianised you, and through them you met and married an honorable man."

"Educated me, forsooth!" she exclaimed with scorn, her nostrils twitching; "they robbed me of my five senses, and gave me instead – accomplishments. Can you tell the time of the day from the sun, sir? Can you say when the sambhur passed whose track is at your feet, and how many wolves were in the pack that followed him? Would your sense of smell lead you to a pool of fresh water in mid-jungle? Can you feel the proximity of a crouching leopard without seeing it? What sort of education is it that neglects the senses? Oh, the highest product of your civilisation – your poet-laureate, Tennyson – felt the same thing stir in his pulses when he wrote 'Locksley Hall,' and deprecated the 'poring over miserable books' with blinded eye-sight."

"'Better fifty years of Europe than a cycle of Cathay,'" I quoted, as she paused in her rapid discourse.

"For the European, perhaps; not for the Chinaman. No, I have no feeling of gratitude towards those you speak of; for the large freedom of the Terai they gave me a brick cage in London; they gave me endless crowds of miserable men and women for these, my green brothers, who are always happy," and she put out her hand and caressed a tree that grew beside her.

"As for Christianity," she resumed, "it is but one facet in the jewel, morality. Christ was but an adept, I take it, who attained to his miraculous powers – as do our rishis and jogis – by prayer and fasting and meditation. I cannot see that Christian vices are fewer or more venial than those of our people."

"But don't you miss your books, and the keeping in touch with the progress of civilisation?" I asked.

"Must I quote 'books in the running brooks' to you? What book is there like this book of God's?" and she swept her arm round her. "And if my son grow up to be brave and strong, that will be civilisation enough for me."

"But your music?"

"Ah! that is the only thing I miss. But I recollect all of Schumann's songs and Schubert's, some of Beethoven's – and then I make songs of my own to fit the moods of my jungle mother, and I have some small skill in weaving words for them."

"And the man who hanged himself?"

"He was no man," she flashed; "who had not the strength of a girl, and who was as weak-eyed as the bat in daytime! You shall see a man indeed, one who fears not to track the tiger afoot, and who even beats me when he sees fit," and she called aloud, "Aho! Kali Dass, aho!"

The sound of the woodman's axe ceased, and presently we heard some one approaching through the jungle. "'Twere better that he should know from me that you and I had had speech together, than that he should learn it from the Terai, for our men are very terrible when they are wrought upon by jealousy." Then, after a pause, she went on, "Don't speak to me in English in his presence. He won't like it."

She rose and half veiled her face with her chudder, as a splendid young Padhan bearing an immense load of wood entered the glade. He threw down his burden as soon as he perceived me, and, snatching up his axe, advanced menacingly towards me. He was a bronze Apollo, with the air of freedom that is native to mountaineers and woodsy folks.

"The sahib intended no harm, Kali Dass," began the woman; "and he hath given me tidings of his death."

"What of it? He was but a quail."

"But now canst thou become a Christian, and – marry me."

"Marry one who was twice a widow? Nana Debi forbid! I must admonish thee when we return to our hut. Come."

Fearing that any further interest in the case on my part would but increase the severity of her punishment, I turned down the jungle path. Just before leaving the glade I looked back; the woman had one knee on the ground, and with outstretched arms she was balancing the load of wood that Kali Dass was putting on her head.

5

A Father Remembers

Extracts from G.R. Kala's *Memoirs of the Raj*

Govind Ram Kala, father of Durga Charan Kala, worked as a civil servant in the Uttar Pradesh government. He began his career in 1911 as a teacher and then sub-deputy inspector of schools. Following a brief stint with the Survey of India he was appointed as a naib tahsildar in 1914 and retired as a deputy collector in 1945. In 1974, at the age of eighty-three, he published *Memoirs of the Raj*, a short book that recalls his many experiences serving under British rule.

While working in Kumaon, G.R. Kala met Jim Corbett on many occasions and writes about his impressions of him, both in Naini Tal and at his winter home of Kaladhungi, where Kala was posted for a time. More interesting and important than his recollections of Corbett, however, are his descriptions of two senior civil servants, Percy Wyndham and A.W. Ibbotson, both of whom were Corbett's close friends. While Kala remembers Corbett as a generous and sympathetic man, who had a sincere concern for the people of Kumaon, his assessment of Wyndham and Ibbotson is more ambivalent. His memoir provides many details about these two men that Corbett's books do not and he offers glimpses into the administrative style of I.C.S. officers who were often accountable only to themselves.

Kala writes in his introduction: "As an underling of the Raj for thirty-one years . . . I had the privilege of watching it closely at the district level and also the men of the Indian Civil Service who headed it. There were some wholly dedicated to the people and others who bided their time hunting and fishing with all the spare time in a more gracious age."

The Bhabar and Terai region of Kumaon served as the venue

for large hunting expeditions that were set up for governors and viceroys. As Kala notes, Jim Corbett was often called upon to organise these shoots. By then he was a well-known shikari and raconteur who had eradicated a number of man-eating tigers and leopards and was much in demand for the stories he had to tell.

These extracts from Kala's book also provide some of the historical context, including the freedom struggle that was beginning to gather force and expressed itself in the Non-Co-operation movement. Pandit Govind Ballabh Pant, the Congress leader from Kumaon, and Sultana Dakku, the infamous bandit, both make an appearance in the memoir. Kala also describes the caste politics, which the British (including Wyndham and Ibbotson) exploited, pitting Brahmins like Kala against Rajput government servants in what is described as a "divide and rule" strategy. He admired yet criticised both these Englishmen and, by his own account, spoke his mind when he felt they were being unfair or prejudiced in their judgements and actions. Wyndham is described as "colourful . . . dour and foul mouthed. . . who spoke the dialect like a native." He employed a retinue of trackers from Mirzapur who had to be kept supplied with country liquor. Ibbotson comes off as a short-tempered and ill-informed man, though ultimately a fair administrator. Both men retired to Kenya in 1947 and (as earlier noted) Corbett went into business with Wyndham, buying coffee estates in East Africa. He also invested in a safari company with Ibbotson. G.R. Kala gives us a unique perspective on the circle of men with whom Corbett associated and, ultimately, his own ambivalent and ambiguous role in the British Raj.

MEMOIRS OF THE RAJ

(Extracts)
Govind Ram Kala
Published by Mukul Prakashan, 1974

Tiger Hunter

Tiger hunting was Mr Wyndham's first love. He spent most of his career hunting either in Mirzapur district (the Wyndham Falls are named after him) or in Naini Tal Tarai. He was Jim Corbett's friend and a colourful person in his own right. He spent 12 years in the Kumaon Division as its Commissioner. He was of medium build, of robust constitution and generally indifferent to his dress. His technique of administration was to strike terror in the hearts of his subordinates. He had a loud voice and he used "damn, silly, hell", his choice epithets, whenever he got an opportunity. Behind the dour exterior, he was a kind man.

Mr Wyndham's capricious ways frightened most people. But the guiding principle of his life, however, was not to deprive anyone of his bread. During the 12 years I served under him, I did not see a single dismissal. Two naib tahsildars, found guilty of bribery and corruption, were reverted to the clerical line but not sacked. Another quality which particularly struck me, was his ability to know personally all his subordinates. He saw through a man and whatever his subordinates did openly or clandestinely never escaped his notice. I know of no Englishman who was so thoroughly informed about the people he worked with.

The Kumaon Commissionership in those days was a sinecure. There was light work and Mr Wyndham devoted all his spare time to hunting. He had his shikaris from his Mirzapur days. As a naib tahsildar, and later as a tahsildar, I had to arrange for young buffaloes, as bait for his tigers. Jim Corbett often accompanied him.

Mr Wyndham never accepted anything from his subordinates. He was honest to the backbone and a staunch opponent of *begar* and *bardaish* which were then in vogue. He raised his voice against this barbarous custom and established what were later known as coolie agencies in Naini Tal district. The full credit for the abolition of the system, however, goes to the Almora Congressmen headed by Pandit Badri Datta Pande, affectionately known as Lattha Pande. In a spectacular act of defiance, he threw all the coolie registers into the Sarju river at the Bageshwar fair in the year 1920.

Mr Wyndham was an astute politician and a perfect master of the divide-and-rule policy. He was the man responsible for creating the Brahmin–Rajput question in Kumaon. He separated the two communities in hostile camps with a careful weightage in jobs. Granted the Rajput was the underdog in the hills under the caste system which acknowledged the superiority of the Brahmin, yet the communities lived in remarkable amity, all sharing the common *hukka* (a great leveler). Mr Wyndham did not like this and set to work inciting the Rajputs against the so-called wrongs done by the Brahmins. Some Garhwal Brahmin officials at Pauri refused to share the *hukka* of a Rajput and this was the small beginning of the question in the early decades of the century.

Thakur Jodh Singh Negi of village Sulla, Narendra Singh Rawat of village Ringwari and Ratan Singh Bisht of village Ophalda soon rose as leaders of the Garhwal Rajputs and started a paper to ventilate the grievances of the community. Some even stopped summoning Brahmins to the smaller religious ceremonies. A general hostility prevailed and Mr Wyndham's efforts widened the split. True, Mr Wyndham wanted recruits for the Army during World War I from among the Rajputs but he could have rewarded them in other ways. The way he split the two communities in the hills will never be forgotten.

Jim Corbett

Jim Corbett, now a famous man after his classic *Man-eaters of Kumaon*, was a resident of Kaladhungi, a small Bhabar town 15 miles away from Naini Tal, where he farmed and did small business in winter when not otherwise gainfully occupied arranging tiger shoots for high-ups in the Government and their guests. Corbett was a constant companion of Mr Wyndham whenever he was out looking for tigers in the Bhabar and Tarai. A bachelor, he lived with his two sisters in a bungalow of his own. He had completely identified himself with the local population which affectionately called him "Carpet Saab". He always had a word of cheer for all those in trouble and was generous with his money. He was quite unlike the general run of the hoity-toity white man. I came in contact with Corbett at Kaladhungi where I was posted as a naib tahsildar in the year 1920–21. He was of middle size and rather dark.

One could see him going about in shorts, shirt, a thick coat of coarse material and a hat. He went about without a tie.

The tahsildars and naib tahsildars of Bhabar and Tarai often came in contact with him for the arrangement of porters and bullock carts for the big shoots. Corbett, of course, was in overall charge of every important shoot. His kindly nature and sympathetic attitude encouraged us to visit him.

Corbett also owned a bungalow at Naini Tal where he lived with his sisters from April to October. Whenever I visited him in Naini Tal, I found his house crowded, so popular was he. He led a simple, unostentatious life. He liked the people of the hills. He would even share their food. During World War I, he raised a labour corps at Bhim Tal and went to France to take active part in the war. The Corbett National Park, named after him, will, however, perpetuate the memory of the famed hunter. He went to Kenya after independence and died there seven years later. It is a pity that he died in a foreign land away from the people he loved so much.

(pp. 19–22)

Corbett's Kaladhungi

Kaladhungi, Jim Corbett's town, is at the foot of the hills. It supported a small permanent population then. The hill people migrated to the town after the Durga Puja for warmth and work and went back after the Holi festival. During the rainy season, the population was appreciably reduced. The hills people could not stand the heat and the malaria. That was long before the World Health Organisation era and the advent of D.D.T.

Even a small town of 500 was enough of a headache. As far as I can recollect, there were about 10 to 12 pucca houses in the town. One head constable was all the police. The non-cooperation movement was at its peak. The slogans of *Bharat Mata Zindabad* and *Angrez Murdabad* rent the sky. The whole atmosphere was charged with anti-British feelings.

People in defiance stopped supplying fuel, grass and milk to the touring Government officers. There were no law courts and no schools at Kaladhungi to be boycotted. There was nothing much of a movement to be carried out, but there was tremendous noise. I found even the simple unsophisticated villager sullen and openly talking against the *Raj.* I soon had a taste of it when I had to make arrangements for the tour of Mr Darling, a member of the Board of Revenue. I had to pay Rs 25 instead of the usual Rs 5 for firewood and the grass for his camp . . . Pandit Govind Ballabh Pant paid a visit to Kaladhungi in connection with his election to the U.P. Legislative Council. We were Kashipur friends and he stayed with me for two days. I did my best to help him. He was returned to the Council.

Sultana Bhantu, the bandit, gave us a scare one night. A rumour spread in the town that Sultana and his gang were due in the evening. The head constable at the police chauki came to me to organise a defence party. We collected some 20 or 30 guns from the neighbouring villages and kept ourselves awake throughout the night. Sultana never harassed Government servants nor did he touch the Government till, otherwise he could have easily looted all the Tarai-Bhabar sub-treasuries which were poorly guarded. The robbers did not turn up that night.

Some Slogans

Mr Wyndham came down to Kaladhungi to watch the non-cooperation movement at close quarters. I met him at the dak bungalow. He expressed a desire to visit the town next day. I warned him the people were rather excited and that it was not desirable for him to visit it in the circumstances. But he would not listen. I brought to his notice the fact that he was in my tashil and I would be held responsible if anything unseemly happened. He reminded me he was the Commissioner and I only a "petty subordinate" who knew nothing about the real state of affairs. I was in a fix. At last I told him that his life and safety were a matter of the greatest importance and though a Commissioner, he should not go against my wishes. But he picked up his hat and stick and started for the town. I had to follow. Not a single person on the way raised his hand to salute him and I knew he would be treated the same way in the town. I again tried to dissuade him but it was all in vain. When we entered the bazaar, none cared to greet him. We made two rounds of the bazaar. No hand was raised in salute and anti-Government slogans were shouted with greater vigour and vehemence. People, apparently unconcerned, smoked, played cards and did the trading. None got up. From Mr Wyndham's face I could well read the situation. He felt greatly humiliated. Later he told me: "Govind Ram, you are a very frank and honest man. What you told me at Kashipur, that every soul was against the Government, that the *Aman Sabhas* were a farce and that the government servants alone stood for the Raj, is correct to the very letter. I am sorry. I did not listen to you. I should have accepted your advice and stayed behind."

I accompanied him back to the dak bungalow. During our conversation, I casually blurted out that he had been unjust to me in getting me superseded twice in my grade promotions in spite of good work. Mr Wyndham was his old self again: "Who says you have done good work? If I say your work is good then it is good and if I say it is bad, then it is bad. Your brain has become heated and I shall take steps to cool it." Cooling came soon in a series of punitive transfers. I had transfers during the next winter to the hills in the cold weather and to the Tarai and Bhabar in summer. I moved like a gypsy from place to place with my wife and children. When I left Champawat for Almora on a transfer, the snow was knee deep. My wife and children experienced considerable suffering in the journey which took five days.

(pp. 62–6)

Unaccounted Expenses

Sir William Marris, Governor of U.P., was now invited by Mr Wyndham to a tiger hunt and I was asked to arrange transport for 20 maunds of luggage from Ramnagar to the hunting camp, some 12 miles away. From past experience, I was certain the luggage would exceed 50 maunds and I manage to hire bullock carts to carry 80.

The day the Governor was to arrive at Ramnagar, Mr Wyndham graciously asked me if I would like to shake hands with the Governor. I had met several Governors and dignitaries by now and shaken hands with them without any particular feeling. . . In the evening, when the Governor came, Mr Wyndham introduced me as the naib tahsildar of Ramnagar and

His Excellency extended his hand. The ceremony over, the Governor and his party got up the elephants and left. The baggage was loaded on camels, which followed. The baggage totaled 100 maunds and the camels had to be loaded rather heavily. The result was that the baggage could not reach the camp before midnight. His Excellency was naturally annoyed and asked the Commissioner to ask for an explanation for the delay. Next day, I received two chits from the Commissioner in one envelope. The upper chit asked me to explain why His Excellency's luggage reached so late. The lower said that I need not be perturbed and could write that the Governor had written he would bring 20 maunds of luggage, whereas he had brought 100 maunds. The explanation satisfied all.

The Governor's camps were expensive affairs. Blocks of ice had to be carted from Ramnagar to the camp every day for chilling the soda and whisky. Country liquor had to be got for the use of the Mirzapur trackers of the Commissioner. Provisions and vegetables were requisitioned daily. The Commissioner had advanced me thousands for the daily expenses. I used to buy the items and record the amount in a notebook. But I was kept so busy that it was impossible to remember every item of expenditure. Many items could not be recorded and accounted for.

His Excellency bagged a tiger and his companions sundry game. The party returned happy to Lucknow. Mr Wyndham asked me to produce the accounts. I told him I had spent all the money advanced by him and that Rs 1,000 could not be accounted for. He took the account sheets from me and distributed Rs 1,000 over various items of expenditure, adding

Rs 200 to a bigger item, Rs 150 to a smaller one and so on. He kindly remarked that neither he nor I had appropriated the money and that it was natural not to record all the items of expenditure while so much had to be done.

(pp. 73–5)

With Ibbotson

I reached Pauri in October 1926 (to work as an assistant record officer under Mr A.W. Ibbotson). Mr Ibbotson was a smallish man with a well-knit body and phenomenal energy. He had distinguished himself in World War I and was awarded the Military Cross. A Senior Wrangler in Mathematics, he could correctly give out the area of a field by walking over its length and breadth. He could frame two scales – one for the area and the other for the assessment rate – in an incredibly short time. According to his own talk, he was one of the Seven Devils of the Indian Civil Service. He was a skilful rider and could cover the distance between Lansdowne and Pauri, some 34 rough miles, in five hours. During his leisure hours, he made rope. He needed no barber. With the help of two mirrors, he could cut his own hair. He also shod his horses himself. Mr Ibbotson was a follower of Mr Wyndham too in his hatred for the Brahmin. But unlike Mr Wyndham, Mr Ibbotson could never hide his strong dislike of the Brahmin community. He was in the hands of a Rajput clique which seized every opportunity to poison his mind against the Brahmins. The leading Congressmen of the district, Pandit Ansuya Prasad Bahugana, Pandit Bhola Datt Chandola and Pandit Vileshwara

Nand Doval were all Brahmins. Pandit Bhola Datt Pant, S.D.M. Pauri, and Lala Prem Lal Sah, A.D.M. also aggravated Mr Ibbotson's hatred by constantly dinning into his ears that the Brahmins of Garhwal were dead set against the Raj.

The settlement operations were started in Pargana Barahsyun first. It took about two years to finish the work. Mr Ibbotson himself wrote the revenue rate report. The Government, however, discovered that it would be a very expensive affair if the whole district was placed under record and settlement operations. In respect of other parganas, the Government wanted to increase the revenue by annas 5 a rupee and assess all the nayaband lands not assessed to revenue previously.

The work was very arduous and I spared no pains. But Mr Ibbotson used to nag and interfere even in insignificant matters. Once an amin, Prasad Singh, fell ill and I had to bring him to my camp for treatment. He requested me to replace him by his son, who was qualified to do the job. I appointed his son and sent the papers to Mr Ibbotson. Someone told him that he was a Brahmin and I was helping one. Mr Ibbotson disapproved of my proposal. I wrote to him, as the survey parties had gone ahead, I could not put off operations just for an amin. Since he was very strict, he ordered me to stick to the orders. I wrote back saying that I was not bound to obey unreasonable orders. He was in a great rage and asked his office to put up the papers at Pauri when I returned from the camp. When Thakur Praduman Singh and I visited his bungalow, the papers were before him. He flared up on seeing me and menacingly raised his fist. Thakur Praduman Singh, a dear friend, got furious and told him that both of us would stand together if he made an attempt to hit me. This had some dampening effect on him. Now started wordy warfare. "How do you dare disobey me?" he growled. In reply, I said: "Ever since I came to serve you, I find that you interfere even in minor details. I am tired of your treatment and would very much like to revert to my original post. Does it befit you to raise your fist against a responsible Government servant? I am not prepared to serve you and you may inform the Government." This made him furious and he picked up his stick to assault me. But Thakur Praduman Singh's warning was still fresh in his mind. I deemed it advisable to get out and went down as far as the public road below his bungalow. Mr Ibbotson followed me shouting all the way. Soon Thakur Praduman Singh followed me. We three were now running, he chasing us both. At last, Mr Ibbotson asked me to stop, saying he meant no harm. I stopped. Mr Ibbotson then addressed me thus: "I lost my temper and it is no credit to me, similarly you lost your temper and it is no credit to you. I shake hands with you and let us forget and forgive the unfortunate incident. I shall never interfere in your work in future, rest assured."

Then I said, having worked in Garhwal district, he should have been aware that the suffix Singh never went with a Brahmin. It was a great shock to him when he learnt he had been misguided. Thakur Pirthi Singh was then the settlement head clerk. He was very competent but an inveterate hater of the Brahmin community. He once took it into his head to lower me in the estimation of Mr Ibbotson by pointing out a flaw in my judgement. This started a pile of correspondence between Mr Ibbotson and myself.

A Long Walk

Once Mr Ibbotson took Thakur Praduman Singh and myself with him to walk some 14 miles from Dogadda to test our physical endurance. We had lunch half way. Both of us were dog tired. Thakur Praduman Singh had a small bottle of brandy and we shared it equally to give us strength to cover the journey. Miss Mayo's *Mother India* was quite a topic those days. The conversation somehow came to it. I had just read the book. Being wiry, I could keep pace with Mr Ibbotson. Thakur Praduman Singh lagged behind. I was a bit relaxed with the brandy and discussed with Mr Ibbotson the undesirability of a publication based on rank falsehood and supported by facts which rarely see the light of day. Mr Ibbotson heard me with attention and at times even encouraged me to speak. When we reached our destination, Mr Ibbotson only remarked: "It's off now." He perhaps meant the discussion.

Mr Ibbotson could take it. The discussion did not warp his judgement about my work. He always made good entries in my character roll every year. One of the great qualities which I found in almost all British I.C.S. officers was that they painted a subordinate as he really was or as they thought he was without allowing any other consideration. They were quick to recognise merits and drawbacks.

(pp. 81–5)

6

"A Place of Proved Desire and Known Delight"

"The Hailey National Park" by D.C. Kala, 27 June 1954

Aside from the two biographies, of Corbett and Frederick Wilson, D.C. Kala also wrote a variety of articles about travel, wildlife, and the Himalaya. Among his papers is a red foolscap register falling apart at the binding and badly mauled by silverfish. Into this lined notebook Kala consigned copies of his shorter pieces, published in a variety of journals, including *The Leader, The Statesman,* and *The Hindustan Times.* Most of these are held in place with rusted paperclips and the yellowed newsprint crumbles at the touch of a finger.

The longest article in this register is an account of a trip that Kala took to India's first National Park in 1954. Founded in 1936, the park was initially named in honour of Sir Malcolm Hailey, then Governor of U.P. Following independence, the name was changed to Ramganga National Park, after the river that runs through the Terai foothills and grasslands. In 1955, once again, the park was renamed, this time as Jim Corbett National Park.

Kala visited the park the year before Corbett died and his description of the forest rest houses and terrain is a fascinating historical record of India's premier tiger reserve. In 1954, hunting was still permitted and the park was ringed by shooting blocks. Kala describes joining a group of shikaris who hunted chital with searchlights. Conservation was still a new concept in India and he bemoans the neglect as well as the terrible roads. The most prescient line of the article warns us: "Too much tourism is as bad for a national park as too little of it." Anyone who has visited Corbett Park in recent years will understand the wisdom in those words.

The Hailey National Park

By D.C. Kala

From *The Hindustan Times Weekly*,
27 June 1954

The Hailey National Park, India's only national park, is languishing for want of care. Roads are in disrepair, some under knee-high shrub, and at least one forest rest house, within the park, once accessible by motor, is not so. Vast herds of cattle graze within the park in clear violation of the U.P. National Parks Act of 1935, exposing deer to cattle disease. Tourist facilities are almost nil, accommodation is uncertain and wild life, after full 18 years of protection, is still too wild because of the continued forestry operations and the heavy shooting on the periphery of the park.

I drove down from Naini Tal one April morning into the humid heat of the Tarai noticing changing wayside vegetation with every thousand feet of elevation lost. I passed Kathgodam, Haldwani and Kaladhungi where Jim Corbett's two derelict houses still stand, and drove into Ramnagar, the railhead, to buy provisions and petrol for the trip.

It was an ordeal doing the shopping in the noon heat in the fly-infested *bazaar*. I took the Ranikhet road and drove for a mile or so and swerved left into the cart track to Bijrani, one entry point to the National Park.

The forest rest house at Bijrani is close to the Ratta Pani Rau and stands on a smallish *chaur* surrounded by hills on three sides. The horizon o

pens west in the direction of the Park gate, if you can call the declivity with the signpost one. You should rather get used to the words, *chaur, rau* and *sot*. The first means a big stretch of grass and the others stand for streams.

Bad Roads

Both the sets in the Rest House were, oddly enough, occupied though I had a permit for one. As the occupants were away at the time, I left the luggage in the car boot and sauntered in the direction of the park gate to stretch my tired bones after a 70-mile gruelling car ride on bad roads. Just beyond the gate, I crossed the Ratta Pani Rau, disturbing a huge flock of parakeets and stood on the bank by a lantana brake to have my first view of the park.

Three sambhar hinds, apparently after quenching their thirst at the Rau, crossed a ridge leisurely into the Bijrani shooting block. A buffalo came down to the water side from the park side, rested awhile on the road, and left for the rest house. Just beyond the Rau, a branch road leads to the hide, erected for wildlife observation. It is an excellent hide and an elaborate affair with a ladder and box on a tree and a neck-high thatch screen. The tree is at the edge of a big *chaur* close to the forest and commands a good view.

As it was dusk, I left the hide and returned to the rest house. On the way I saw a very fresh pugmark of a smallish tiger on the dust of the road. It was not there when I passed the spot on my way to the hide. I looked carefully for the tiger right up to the edge of the jungle to my right but without luck. Was it after the buffalo?

Back at the rest house, the problem of accommodation was amicably settled in my absence, a kind forest officer having offered to put us up with him at considerable inconvenience to himself.

Hunter's Party

That night, after an early dinner, I joined a hunter's party, bristling with rifles and searchlights, and drove to the rest house at Malani and back. The Malani–Bijrani road is part of the southern boundary of the park and is very much in use for hunting.

The headlights of the pick-up lit up the greenish eyes of chital resting by the wayside. The headlights immobilised the whole herd and every deer seemed to be looking at us with expectancy. The hunter with the searchlight brought the pick-up to a halt with two sharp raps on the hood of the vehicle and brought the searchlight into play. The beam stopped at a stag. "Forty inches," whispered his friend. "Let's have him." Karrarak boom, the rifle spat. There was a stampede in the bush, the greenish lights went off and a man jumped down to cut the stag's throat and seek the benediction of God. I helped to load the stag into the vehicle and noticed with distaste that it was in velvet.

A mile ahead we passed a sambhar herd grazing by the roadside. The searchlight made no impression on them too, at least two continued to graze in unconcern. The return drive was uneventful except for a hog deer that crossed the road into the Malani Sot with its muzzle well down and a hare that ran in the blaze of the headlights for half a mile.

Night at Rest House

Back at Bijrani, I settled down in a cot for the night under the verandah roof to the racket of the *sweesh chweep* of the Franklin's night-jar and the hammer-on-wood *tough tough* of its long-tailed cousin. Far away a peafowl meowed, a kakar barked in the Bijrani shooting black and two lapwings flew over the rest house calling to each other. "Did he do it? Did he do it?"

The next morning I rose to the cheeping of a purple sunbird on the creeper at the edge of the verandah and the liquid musical notes of the golden oriole perched on a leafing silk cotton tree, long past its flowering prime, and walked to the hide. I spent two rather fruitless hours there hearing barbets, coppersmiths and doves sing and watching the antics of three bee-eaters making sorties at whatever they were after, from the stump of a tree below.

At nine, a small chital herd descended the hillock opposite the hide into a reintrant [*sic*] well under cover. They were rather nervous the way they crossed an open space between two clumps of sal.

After lunch I accompanied a movie man to a small lake in the Malani shooting block in the expectation of seeing a tiger. A four-hour vigil on the mosquito-infested mulchy bank yielded no tiger though hopes rose high once when a langur, up on the ridge called *khok khok khok khokorror* and a sisterhood of laughing thrushes took up the alarm with their vehement *whak whaks*.

The short-lived excitement over, the waterfront grew quiet except for the feeding fish, the patter of falling sal flowers on the dry leaves of the forest floor, the kingfisher that returned to the bough overhanging the lake with a jubilant *klee klee* whenever it made a kill, the bee-eaters picking dragon flies skimming on the surface of the lake and the two lapwings that dipped their beaks deep into the mulch of the lake and let go an occasional *tut tut* at us.

Swampy Region

Because of the stretch of the road that connects Malani, Janagwar Gaujpani and Patairpani not being motorable throughout, I had to take a roundabout route to enter the park again. I drove to Garjia and stayed there for two nights to visit Sitabani, a very interesting place with a fresh water swamp and a big stream coming out of it. Garjia was once famous for its fishing, but it has been all but ruined by the heavy diversion of the waters of the Kosi into the canals down below and the heavy poaching. I heard the Indian cuckoo there and the fireflies were something new to watch by night.

I took the Ranikhet road again and entered the park by the Dhangarhi Gate. There is a proper locked gate here and the keeper had to be roused from slumber because of the early hour. I by-passed the rest house at Sultan, a drab place in the sal forest, and drove to Sarapduli on the Ramganga. Sarapduli was also famous for fishing in the river judging from the exploits and comments of visiting anglers in the visitors' book. But the fishing, it is claimed by the Forest Department, is being seriously menaced by crocodiles and otters. I read an appeal to all hunters to co-operate in their destruction. How much of this recent increase in their numbers and the poor fishing is due to the dam built 20 miles below the park on the Ramganga is worth investigation.

The keeper was away with the key and I managed a back-door entry into the rest house. An hour later, he arrived with a pail of milk got for us from a place seven miles away to be sold at the market rate. This is one incident to prove the proverbial hospitality of the Forest Department. As I had plenty of milk-powder, I spared the man who brought it, the daily 14-mile walk.

Jungle Spring

Below Sarapduli, which literally means snake's hole, the Patli Dun Valley of the Ramganga begins. It terminates 15 miles below near Boxar and is famed for its jungle spring. The flowering cycle begins with the blood-red flowers of the silk cotton, the scarlet and orange flowers of the dhak and the white, pink and purple flowers of the kachnar. It ends with the white flowers of the sandan, the whitish ones of kumbhi and sal, and the yellow foot-long sprigs of the amaltas. I was a bit late for the peak jungle spring but was eminently satisfied with the shisham trees under new leaf in the river terraces, the few dhaks still flowering and pink kusum trees in the Ramganga gorge. Among shrubs, the small star-shaped flowers of the karonda were most aromatic.

Ornithologically, Sarapduli was interesting for the morning song of the mountain thrush and the din raised by a colony of very vociferous hawk cuckoos. I particularly remember a hoarse-throated one that exercised its vocal cords sometimes far into the night.

After a memorable lunch, made so because of a welcome change provided by wild gular figs over the eternal potato and onion, and a two-hour snooze, I drove to Dhikala to meet the Divisional Forest officer of Kalagarh who happened to be camping there and heard from him the progress made by him with an artificial salt lick on the chaur there. I spent an hour in the hide there. It was a fruitless hour but for the fact that on the bottom boards of the hide I noticed three oily patches where a bear had rested his two sweaty paws and a very sweaty posterior.

Linlithgow's Remarks

At the rest house, I went over the visitors' book and read Linlithgow's remark written in 1940 after catching a 36 ½ lb. mahseer. "A place of proved desire and known delight," he wrote. "Met tiger broad daylight," wrote another.

The book had a very amusing entry from a Conservator of Forests on a divisional forest officer put on the carpet for mistakenly shooting a tiger within the boundary of the park. He thought it fit to reprimand the officer in the visitors' book, a book open to the public.

The chaur at Dhikala extends right up to Boxar and sustains a vast herd of cattle. The rest house faces a river terrace under clumps of shisham.

I had to change plans on being informed that the rest house at Boxar, which I was due to occupy after two days, would not be available and secured permission to go to Patairpani, the last rest house accessible by motor well within the park. I drove back at eight at night to Sarapduli.

Sarapduli, I was told, is the easternmost limit of the wandering elephant herds. The Champion Pool, a little below the ford opposite the rest house, is worth a visit. There, a chital hind, acting as sentry to a small watering herd, called at me for full five minutes and a pig, also watering there, showed unbelievable speed on spotting me. The Champion road, that leads to the pool, is under knee-high scrub.

The next morning I drove to Patairpani past the chaur of Dhikala, the grass golden under the morning sun. Instead of taking the regular road via Boxar, I took the Sambhar Road. It is well within the forest. Here I got the few thrills of the park of seeing deer and pig almost blocking the road. We had to stop at least twice to get our right of way and when the right was finally given, we were kept under watch for quite some time. Due to some inexplicable reason, the park deer seemed tolerant of the car but not so of the man on foot. I had the occasion to check this on Sambhar Road.

Awful Journey

I by-passed Boxar and managed to reach Patairpani after an awful journey on a newly repaired road in which the car sank right up to the axle at least at three places. The keeper was away and the driver, an excellent mechanic, showed his skill at house-breaking again without as much as scratching a door. At noon, however, I got a pail of milk and a chit from Boxar that the keeper would be there by sundown and he did reach before that.

A huge forest fire, that blazed for at least three days, ruined my stay there for wildlife simply vanished from the area. For three days I watched the clumsy efforts at controlling the fire with a single truck, that too luckily available from a touring forest officer. A major portion of the south-western corner of the park was gutted in that fire. I cannot imagine the loss to wildlife that perished within when the counter-fires were started to localise the main fire.

The rest house stands on a knoll in undulating country. Just below is the marsh with its edible ferns – young shoots only mind you.

I did not go to the hide there with the "best view in western circle" and instead devoted a whole evening to the Patairpani Rau with its maze of tiger, deer and elephant tracks. Here I discovered the first ant-lion of the park and counted at least six species of fish fingerlings in a small pool. I saw two black partridges fighting and peacock in mating display.

After staying for two days at Patairpani, I drove to Boxar. It has another big chaur and another herd of cattle. On the way I saw a sambhar hind and fawn feeding on a low bough at the roadside. They let the car pass in unconcern, watched us stop, and then again in unconcern turned to the bough to tear juicy morsels. The fawn had a silly face and outsize ears.

I was hard-pressed for time, so did not stop at Boxar and drove straight to Kalagarh on one of the most dangerous roads I have ever seen. It hugged the Ramganga gorge, the river foaming below.

At Kalagarh, I said goodbye to the park and took the road to Ramnagar. Though I saw no tiger, no bear, no wild elephant, no wild dog, no python, no crocodile and no otter within it, it was a great experience.

Tourism Development

Too much tourism is as bad for a national park as too little of it. Indeed the very existence of this 125 sq. miles park in the Himalayan foothills of UP remains unknown to millions. Serious efforts should now be made by a proper, logical and scenic survey and improvement of roads, a Bijrani to Boxar motor road to be the first priority. At rest houses, cooking utensils and crockery should be kept for the convenience of tourists. In some key rest houses khansamas should be kept. A State-run hotel can be maintained as is being done in the Periyar Sanctuary by the Travancore Cochin Government, the hotel to provide transport to and from the railheads at Kotdwara and Ramnagar. Dual control of the Park – it is under two divisions, each responsible for its own area – should end. Guides should be provided as the forest guard is a poor substitute. And elephants should be maintained for transport. Private enterprise should be encouraged to arrange conducted tours and other connected activities if the State Government is indifferent.

Though the National Park was set up in 1935 under the UP National Parks Act and wildlife has been given full 18 years of protection, it is incomprehensible why it should continue to be so wild all along the main roads. Though the higher forest brass outright denied the existence of poaching, the underdogs of the department in everyday contact with the Park, did not deny it.

7

Final Instructions

The Last Will and Testament of Jim Corbett

Reading someone's Last Will and Testament is usually of little interest to anyone except those who may have been remembered and rewarded with a bequest, but Jim Corbett's Will is a fascinating document for several reasons. First and foremost, it provides evidence of his thoughtful, fastidious nature, which comes through in his books as well as his methods of hunting and photography. Very little is left to chance, and as he approaches the end of his life Corbett apportions his estate with precise and carefully considered instructions.

Of course, his sister Maggie is the primary beneficiary, along with a number of other family members scattered around the globe. His editors and publishers at Oxford University Press – R.E. Hawkins in Bombay, Geoffrey Cumberlege in London, and Henry Z. Walck in New York – receive antique carpets and a tiger skin as a sign of Corbett's gratitude. He had earlier gifted his prized .275 Rigby Mauser rifle, presented to him by the Lt Governor of the United Provinces after he killed the man-eater of Champawat, to the Oxford University Press, where it must have been received with bewilderment. More than likely this is the only instance in which an author thanked his publishers by giving them a gun. Some years later, OUP faced an embarrassing situation when the police confiscated the weapon because they didn't have a valid licence.

One of the interesting bequests in this Will is granted to the Duke of Edinburgh, whom Corbett addresses with all of the formality and deference of a dyed-in-the-wool royalist that he was. Having recently met Princess Elizabeth and Prince Philip at Tree Tops Hotel in Kenya, Corbett was a great fan of the young queen and her consort. He left a thousand pounds sterling to the Playing Fields Association of England, of which the Duke was a patron, "as a token of my gratitude for the kindness shewn to me by Her Majesty the Queen and His Royal Highness at Treetops." Underscoring his interest in sports and physical fitness, Corbett also left five hundred pounds to construct a playing field in his adopted home of Nyeri and specified that it was to be "for the use of persons of all races."

Most of the man-eater trophies were auctioned off by his executors, the Standard Bank of South Africa, and the proceeds were distributed to support institutions that educated and cared for the blind. St Dunstan's Institute for the Blind was one of the beneficiaries and Corbett obviously felt a great sense of compassion for those who had lost their sight. A portion of the royalties from *Man-Eaters of Kumaon* had earlier been assigned to St Dunstan's to support the treatment and rehabilitation of soldiers who had been blinded during the two world wars. Above all else, Corbett's Will provides an intimate glimpse into the mind of a man preparing for death. As Maggie tells us, his health had been poor since leaving India. Though he was not a wealthy man, Corbett had accumulated a sizeable estate for someone who came from very humble beginnings and, as he listed the various bequests, his natural kindness and generosity shows through the convoluted and archaic language of this legal document.

F 43

P.&A. No. 10
COLONY AND PROTECTORATE OF KENYA

IN HER MAJESTY'S SUPREME COURT AT NAIROBI

PROBATE AND ADMINISTRATION

Cause No. 299 of 1955

Probate of the Will of **Edward James Corbett**
deceased
who died on the **19th** day of **April 1955**
at **Nyeri, in the colony of Kenya**

Be it known that on the **3rd** day of **December,** in the year 1955 the last Will of **Edward James Corbett** late of **Nyeri aforesaid** a copy of such Will here annexed, was proved and registered before me, and that the Administration of the Property and Credits of the said deceased and in any way concerning his Will was granted to **The Standard Bank of South Africa, Nairobi**

-- the

executor in the

said Will named, they having undertaken well and faithfully to administer the same and to make a full and true inventory of the Property and Credits and to exhibit the same in this Court within six months from the date of this grant or within such further time as the Court may from time to time appoint, and also to render to this Court a true account of the said Property and Credits within one year from the said date or within such further time as the Court may from time to time appoint.

. . . by her Majesty's Supreme Court at **Nairobi** . . .
3rd day of **December . . . .** 1955.
G.B. Rudd
JUDGE,
SUPREME COURT OF KENYA

This is the last Will of me

EDWARD JAMES CORBETT of the Outspan Hotel Nyeri in the Central Province of the Colony of Kenya a Lieutenant Colonel (Retired) in her Majesty's Army which I make on this Twenty First day of May One thousand nine hundred and fifty four.

1. I HEREBY REVOKE all testamentary dispositions heretofore made by me.
2. I DECLARE that inasmuch as I have relinquished my domicile of origin and have acquired a domicile of choice in the said Colony of Kenya and have no choice in the said Colony of Kenya and have no intention of changing such domicile it is my wish and intention that this my Will and any codicil which I may make hereto shall be construed and take effect in all respects according to the law of the said Colony.
3. I APPOINT THE STANDARD BANK OF SOUTH AFRICA LIMITED (hereinafter called "the Bank") to

be executor and trustee of this my will on the Bank's published terms and conditions including those relating to the right to remuneration and the incidence of such remuneration as set forth therein as if such terms and conditions were herein declared save that the amount of the remuneration from time to time payable to the Bank shall be calculated in accordance with the Bank's charges ruling at the date when the Bank commences its duties hereunder.

4. I DESIRE that the Advocates if any to be employed in connection with my estate will if possible be MESSIEURS R.A. LITTLE AND COMPANY of Nyeri aforesaid but without prejudice to the right of the Bank to consult or employ any other legal advisers in any case in which it shall think fit so to do at the expense of my estate.

5. I GIVE AND BEQUEATH all my estate both real and personal whatsoever and wheresoever situate of which I shall die possessed after payment thereout of my just debts funeral and testamentary expenses and death duties of whatever nature soever payable in respect of any legacies hereby or by any codicil hereto bequeathed free of duty unto the Bank upon the following trusts:-

   (a) As to the income thereof unto my sister MARGARET WINIFRED CORBETT of the Outspan Hotel aforesaid during her life AND I EMPOWER my said sister at any time or times to require in writing the Bank to sell any part or parts of the capital of my estate either real or personal and to pay the proceeds of sale to her for her own absolute use AND I DIRECT the Bank to carry out her written wishes in this behalf;

(b) SUBJECT thereto I GIVE AND BEQUEATH freed and discharged from all death duties of whatever nature soever absolutely:-

   (1) UNTO my nephew DOUGLAS CORBETT of Number 29 Victoria Road New Barnet in the County of Herford in England the original manuscripts of all books written by me my painted glazed miniature and my medals now held in safe custody by the Bank with the request that they be retained in the Corbett family and I direct the Bank to be responsible for the cost of packing freight insurance and other like charges thereon out of the residue of my estate.

   (2) UNTO my good friend GEOFFREY CUMBERLEGE of the Oxford University Press Amen House Warwick Square in the City of London as a token of my affection and regard for all his kindness to my said sister and to myself the larger of the two carpets belonging to me and now in my bedroom at the Outspan Hotel aforesaid such carpet measuring eight feet by seven feet and made in India over a hundred years ago and I direct the Bank to pack the same in a tin-lined case created to avoid damage in transit and to be responsible

for the cost of packing freight insurance and other like charges thereon out of the residue of my estate.

(3) UNTO my good friend R.E. HAWKINS of the Oxford University Press aforesaid as a token of my affection and regard for all his kindness to my said sister and myself the smaller of the said two carpets belonging to me measuring nine feet by five feet and made in Shiraz and my nine illustrated volumes of Shakespeare and I direct the Bank to pack the same in a tin-lined case crated to avoid damage in transit and to be responsible for the cost of packing freight insurance and other like charges out of the residue of my estate.

(4) UNTO my good friend HENRY Z. WALCK of the Oxford University Press Number 114 Fifth Avenue New York 11 in the United States of America as a token of my affection and regard for all his kindness to my said sister and to myself the tiger skin of "The Bachelor of Powalgarh" and I direct the Bank to pack the same in a tin-lined case crated to avoid damage in transit and to be responsible for the cost of packing freight insurance and other like charges out of the residue of my estate.

(5) UNTO Colonel JEFFREY LINCOLN-GORDON of the Maragua Fort Hall in the

Central Province of the said Colony such of my clothing as he may care to have.

(6) UNTO my nephew General THOMAS WILLIAM CORBETT of Mweiga in the Central Province of the said Colony such of my pictures and books as he may care to have.

(7) UNTO the GOVERNOR of the Colony of Kenya for the benefit of blind Africans in the said Colony one moiety of the net proceeds of sale of all my man-eater and other skins not hereby or by any codicil hereto specifically bequeathed and I direct that the Bank shall sell such skins by public auction in Nairobi.

(8) UNTO the GOVERNOR of the Province of Uttar Pradesh in India for the benefit of the blind of the District of Kumaon the other moiety of such proceeds for sale.

(9) UNTO PRISCILLA CORBETT daughter of my nephew the said General Thomas William Corbett upon her attaining the age of twenty one years or previously marrying the sum of Five hundred pounds sterling.

(10) UNTO the Nairobi Branch of THE SALVATION ARMY for its Eventide Homes the sum of Two hundred pounds sterling.

(11) UNTO the Nairobi Branch of ST DUNSTAN'S INSTITUTE FOR THE BLIND the sum of Two hundred pounds sterling.

(12) UNTO THE BOY SCOUTS ASSOCIATION OF KENYA the sum of One hundred pounds sterling.

(13) UNTO THE GIRL GUIDES ASSOCIATION OF KENYA the sum of One hundred pounds sterling.

(14) UNTO THE MOUNT KENYA HOSPITAL of Nyeri aforesaid the sum of Two hundred pounds sterling.

(15) UNTO the PROVINCIAL COMMISSIONER of the Central Province of the said Colony the sum of Five hundred pounds sterling to provide a playing field at Nyeri aforesaid for the use of persons of all races.

(16) UNTO the NYERI ENGLISH CHAPLANCY FUND the sum of One hundred pounds sterling to be used for repairing or furnishing St Cuthbert's Church in Nyeri.

(17) UNTO my nephew RAY NESTOR and his wife DOROTHY jointly or the survivor of them as the case may be of Number 10 Emerson Court Wimbledon Hall Road London S.W. 19 the sum of One thousand pounds sterling.

(18) UNTO my nephew ST ELMO HASLETT of the China Coast Officers' Club King's Buildings Connaught Road Central Hongkong in the Colony of Hongkong the sum of One thousand pounds sterling.

(19) UNTO ST DUNSTAN'S INSTITUTE FOR THE BLIND of Number 1 South Audley Street in the City of Westminster in England the sum of One thousand pounds sterling.

(20) UNTO DAVID WOODWARD of Sans Pareil Ooan Road Rondebosch Capetown in the Union of South Africa the sum of One thousand pounds sterling in gratitude for his kindness to my brother John and his wife Kathleen.

(21) UNTO His Royal Highness THE DUKE OF EDINBURGH for the Playing Fields Association of England the sum of One thousand pounds sterling which with my respectful loyalty I beg that His Royal Highness will be graciously pleased to accept as a token of my gratitude for the kindness shewn to me by Her Majesty the Queen and His Royal Highness at Treetops Nyeri aforesaid.

(22) UNTO my grandnephew GEORGE MARSHALL the sum of One thousand pounds sterling to enable him to further his studies at the school for the blind.

(23) UNTO my nephew DOUGLAS CORBETT and his wife SAIDI jointly or the survivor of them as the case may be the sum of One thousand pounds sterling.

(24) UNTO my niece DOROTHY LINCOLN-GORDON of Maragua Fort Hall aforesaid

and her husband the said Colonel Jeffrey Lincoln-Gordon jointly or the survivor of them an annuity to be purchased by the Bank for the purchase price of One thousand pounds from the Nairobi Branch of the Manufacturer's Life Insurance Company of Canada.

(25) UNTO my niece VIVIAN STUTCHBURY of Number 5 Burdon Hall Eashing near Godalming in the County of Surrey in England an annuity to be purchased by the Bank for the purchase price of Five hundred pounds from the Nairobi Branch of the Manufacturer's Life Insurance Company of Canada.

(26) UNTO ST DUNSTAN'S INSTITUTE FOR THE BLIND of Number 1 South Audley Street aforesaid my said grandnephew GEORGE MARSHALL and THE OXFORD UNIVERSITY PRESS of Amen House Warwick Square aforesaid (for their private charities as a token of gratitude for their kindness to my said sister and myself) in equal shares all the royalties and other income from my books actually received after the date of the death of the survivor of my said sister and myself such income to be collected by the said Oxford University Press and disposed of in accordance with the provisions of this clause.

(27) UNTO such of my grandnephews and grandniece and of the children of my nephew the

said Douglas Corbett as shall survive the survivor of my said sister and myself and if more than one in equal shares all the residue of my estate both real and personal whatsoever and wheresover situate of which I shall die possessed after payment thereout of all such packing freight and insurance and other like charges as aforesaid.

6. I DECLARE that in the case of bequests to institutions made hereby or by any codicil hereto the receipt of the Treasurer or Secretary or any other responsible officer of such institution shall be a sufficient discharge unto the Bank and that the Bank shall not be concerned in any way with the application of the monies comprising such bequests.
7. I DECLARE that in the event of my having made and informed the Bank in writing of any gift during my lifetime corresponding with or exceeding any bequest to the same person or persons institution or institutions herein contained or in any codicil hereto contained then such bequest shall thereupon become void and of no effect and similarly in the event of my having made and informed the Bank in writing of any such gift as aforesaid of lesser amount than the corresponding bequest then such bequest shall abate proportionately as if the difference between such gift and such bequest only had been specifically bequeathed hereby or by any codicil hereto.
8. I DECLARE that whereas I am now possessed of assets in the United Kingdom and in India and in Africa

I desire that the bequests (if any) contained herein or in any codicil hereto made in rupee currency should as far as practicable be satisfied from my Indian assets and that similarly such bequests made to persons or institutions in Africa should be satisfied from my assets in the United Kingdom provided nevertheless that the Bank shall not be bound by this my desire if for any reason compliance therewith should not prove to be convenient or practicable.

9. I DESIRE that if practicable my body shall be cremated.

IN WITNESS whereof I have hereunto set my hand the day and year first above written.

Signed by the said
Edward James Corbett J. Corbett
as his last Will and
Testament in the presence
of us both being present
at the same time who at
his request and in such
joint presence as afore-
said have hereunto subscribed
our names as witnesses:-

R.A. Little Advocate, Nyeri
S. Wilson Secretary, Nyeri

Afterword
The Hunter as Author

STEPHEN ALTER

Very little remains to be written about Jim Corbett that hasn't been written already. He was an anomaly of the British Raj; one of the few Englishmen that lived in India before independence who is still remembered with admiration as well as some affection. While the statues of his fellow colonials were all pulled down soon after 1947, several busts of Corbett have been erected in his honour following independence, including one at the gate of the national park that bears his name. Placed on a cracked masonry pedestal, it is a poor likeness that bears a pained expression, as if he would rather not have been recognised in this manner. Though Corbett seldom wore a tie, especially not in the jungle, the sculptor has knotted one at his throat and he looks a bit like a trophy head on display.

Numerous tributes have been printed over the years, from formal citations issued by viceroys and governors who praised Corbett's skills as a slayer of man-eaters to awestruck essays by schoolchildren hailing his more benevolent role as a conservationist. The Internet, which has become our primary source of information for better or worse (usually the latter), is cluttered with hagiographies and half-truths that tell us little about the man and more about how he has been reimagined as an iconic hunter and naturalist prowling the treacherous jungles of Cyberspace.

The seven documents in this book were all written more than forty years ago, before computers took over the world. In the case of Corbett's first book, *Jungle Stories*, it was composed in 1935 using lead type and set by hand on a Letterpress machine, then printed one page at a time. Running your fingers over the text, you can feel the bite of the words on paper, as if it were braille. D.C. Kala's biography was written in the 1970s on a manual typewriter that had jammed, producing only capital letters. Meanwhile, around the same time, his father, Govind Ram Kala, recorded his memories of Corbett, Wyndham, and Ibbotson in a foolscap ledger. And Ruby Beyts' faithful transcription of her interviews with Maggie, from the early 1960s, are preserved in faint type that looks as if it might be a carbon copy. Surprisingly, the oldest document, Charles Doyle's novel, *The Taming of the Jungle,* which came out in 1899, is the most legible of all, though the book itself – an American edition, discarded by the St Johnsburg Athanaeum in Vermont – is dog-eared and coming apart at the binding, its spine reinforced with Scotch Tape. The final document, Corbett's Will, written in 1954, a year before his death, is an attested "True Copy" reproduced on a Photostat machine and impressed with a Notary's seal.

In many ways, the first drafts of Corbett's books consisted of his letters to Maggie, written while he was camped in the jungle. These were carried back by a mail runner to Nainital or Kaladhungi. A few of the original letters have survived, mostly in the archives of the Oxford University Press. Perhaps the most interesting of all were those written while he was hunting the Chowgarh man-eater, an animal that proved particularly elusive and whose tale is recounted in *Jungle Stories*. As several researchers have pointed out, including the authors of *Behind Jim Corbett's Stories Vol. 2,* from which the extracts below have been quoted, a few noticeable discrepancies exist between his letters to Maggie and the stories as they finally appeared in print. It is unclear whether Corbett referred to the letters when writing his book but it is reasonable to assume that with the passage of time his memories may not have been precise. An author of hunting yarns must also be permitted some literary licence when retelling a complex and exciting tale.

In a letter written on 10 April 1930, he expresses his frustration to Maggie at not being able to track down the Chowgarh man-eater:

> It takes a lot to discourage me but I was beginning to feel that it is hopeless trying to get a shot at the tigress. She is very restless at this time of the year and has such a lot of country to wander over that it is almost impossible to locate her. I have put fresh earth in dozens of places on the roads but she prefers to keep to the jungle and so far I have not seen her prints. Another thing, unless her kills are in thick cover she won't return to them.

After writing these words, on the very next day, 11 April 1930, he comes upon the tigress almost by accident and finally puts an end to her career. Again, Maggie is the first to hear the news from Jim:

> Just a line to let you know that I shot the man-eater at 5 this evening. I will tell you all about it when I get home. It will take a couple of days to dry the skin and if today is Friday as Ganga Ram says it is, I will start on Monday and be at home on Tuesday night – but don't worry if I fail to turn up on Tuesday. I might be delayed over the skin. It has taken some getting and I don't want to risk its getting spoilt.
>
> On second thought I think I had better give you a brief account of what actually happened this evening, for from the scraps of conversation I heard before dinner, the story, although

only three hours old, is already badly distorted, and will be unrecognisable by the time it gets to Naini, per the bearer of this.

At three o'clock this afternoon I set out to tie a katra up at Saryapani where I had been tying up since the 31st.[1] On the way out I changed my mind and instead of going to Saryapani turned down the forest track with the intention of tying the katra up where the Chamoli boy was killed on the 25th February. Most of the jungle had been burnt out but about half a mile down the track I came on a nice bit of green grass on which several sambhar were feeding. It looked as good a place as any so I made the men (I had three with me) collect a few bundles of oak leaves, and before leaving the katra I made a man go up a tree growing on the edge of the Khud and call, as they do here when out with cattle. I, in the meantime, stood on a projecting rock nearby and once I thought I heard a movement down below me but could not be sure. Anyway the men had heard nothing so we left the katra, to go up the zig zag track to Dharampani where the Vivians and I had sat one evening looking down the valley. After going a few yards I came to a deep nala. As it looked a likely place for tracks I climbed down into it and found the tracks of the man-eater. The tracks were old, possibly made by the tiger when going away after eating out Vivian's katra. Anyway I decided to go down the nala and look for tracks where it joined the main ravine. The going was bad over huge rocks and in one place I wanted a free hand. By the way, I have forgotten to mention that I picked up two nightjar's eggs close to where the katra was tied so I handed the rifle to Madho Singh. I got down alright and as Madho Singh joined me he put the rifle in my right hand, I had the eggs in the other, and whispered

[1] Katra: Young male buffalo.

> that some animal had growled like a pig or a bear, he was not sure which. The nala was very narrow just here, to our right and overhanging us was an enormous rock the top of which was about eight feet above our heads. At the lower end of the rock the bed of the nala was on a level with the banks. I tip-toed forward without making a sound and as I cleared the rock I looked over my right shoulder and – looked straight into the tiger's face. She flattened down her ears and bared her teeth and slipped forward but by then I had slipped the safety over and the bullet went through her heart. It was all over in a heartbeat and the tiger was dead as nails. I am glad I got her like this – no sitting up and no fuss. She was just what I expected her to be – old and thin, cracked pads and teeth worn down to the gums, but her coat, on the whole is not bad. I told Vivian last year that she was 8 – 4. I might be an inch out – no more. I did not break the eggs and the Nightjar was glad to get them back.
>
> Pass the news on to Vivian and Stiffe, they will be relieved to know that the Chowgarh man-eater is dead.[2]

Corbett anticipated some of his readers questioning the authenticity of his stories, particularly incidents such as the shooting of the Chowgarh tigress, aiming and firing his rifle with one hand while holding a clutch of nightjar eggs in the other. In a note written after the publication of *Man-Eaters of Kumaon,* he insists that he has always been able to depend on his memory because of his own observant nature. "I am confident that if you were to question me tomorrow, or ten years hence, I would from memory be able to retell the story of the nightjar,

[2] Preetum Gheerawo, "The Chowgarh Letters and Other Material", *Behind Jim Corbett's Stories, Vol. 2.* pp. 206–7.

word for word, as I have told it above. And this cannot be attributed to my mind being young and receptive; but it can be attributed to my having taken an interest in the scene which is now indelibly etched in my memory."[3]

More than his books, Corbett's most important legacy is the way in which his stories of jungle lore have inspired a number of conservationists. Just one example is Dr A.J.T. Johnsingh, among India's foremost experts on wildlife, who worked for many years at the Wildlife Institute of India in Dehradun and retired from there as a Dean of Faculty. In a memoir titled *On Jim Corbett's Trail,* Johnsingh describes how, as a young boy, living in a small town in South India he "accidentally discovered a Tamil translation of Jim Corbett's *Man-eaters of Kumaon.* I came upon the book on the wrong shelf in a corner of the library. As I greedily turned its pages it cast a spell on me that still has not lifted."[4]

Many years later, in 1993, Johnsingh and his colleague at WII, Dr G.S. Rawat, revisited many of the places that Corbett describes in his books. They travelled from Kaladhungi to Mukteshwar, Devidhura, Champawat, Thak, and Chuka, finally passing below the Purnagiri Temple on their way down to Tanakpur. As wildlife scientists they took note of the dramatic changes in the ecology of the region, especially the

[3] Jim Corbett, *My Kumaon: Uncollected Writings*. Delhi: Oxford University Press, 2012, p. 7.

[4] A.J.T. Johnsingh, *On Jim Corbett's Trail*, Delhi: Permanent Black, 2004.

disappearance of mammals such as sambhar and tigers, which were once commonly found in the hills of Kumaon.

Corbett's books have a way of inspiring his readers to seek out the landscapes and landmarks he describes. It may be his detailed and specific accounts of the physical world or the powerful, underlying sense of place his words evoke, but I myself remember being drawn into a quest to retrace his footsteps. In 1979, accompanied by a close friend and photographer, Gurmeet Thukral, I trekked along most of the same route that Johnsingh and G.S. Rawat followed a couple of decades later. I remember that trip as a remarkable adventure and an account of our trek was published in *The Illustrated Weekly of India*. We started by walking up the old path from Corbett's home in Kaladhungi to Nainital, where we paid our respects at Gurney House and then set off eastward to Mornala and Devidhura, where we ascended a path that Corbett describes in *The Temple Tiger*. "The western approach to Dabidhura [*sic*] is up one of the steepest roads in Kumaon. The object of the man who designed this road . . . was to get to the top by the shortest route possible, and this he accomplished by dispensing with hairpin bends and running his road straight up the face of the 8,000 foot mountain."[5] Years later, I still have a clear memory of that near-vertical section of the trek, as well as the ache in my legs and the utter exhaustion I felt when we finally reached the top. But, of course, I was in my twenties then and anything was possible. I can also

[5] Jim Corbett, *The Temple Tiger*, London: Oxford University Press, 1955, p. 7.

recall spending a night at the foot of Purnagiri and fruitlessly scanning the dark profiles of surrounding mountains in the hope of seeing the sacred lights described in *Jungle Stories*.

But of all those who have tracked down the sites where Corbett hunted his man-eaters and identified specific rocks and ridgelines, there is no more devoted fraternity than the authors of a two-volume epic, *Behind Jim Corbett's Stories: An Analytical Journey to "Corbett's Places" and Unanswered Questions.* For more than a decade these dedicated researchers have made regular visits to Kumaon and searched out the exact locations where Corbett lay in wait for his tigers or followed their pugmarks into sandy ravines. Just as devotees of James Joyce walk the streets of Dublin with his novels in hand, these Corbett aficionados refer to his books as if they were a literary GPS. Another remarkable aspect of this team of five men is that they come from five different continents and are drawn together by a single obsession – to corroborate Corbett's written record of events and terrain.[6]

The true test of any author's work is its longevity. The fact that Corbett's books have remained popular well beyond his lifetime, and have now entered the public domain with a new generation of readers eager to let his words transport them back to the jungles of India, speaks to the enduring quality of his writing with its compelling narratives and vivid imagery.

[6] These five individuals are Priyavrat Gadhvi, Preetum Gheerawo, Manfred Waltl, Joseph Jordania, Fernando Quevedo de Oliveira. Stuart Gelzer also accompanied the team and contributed to Volume 2.

This collection is an effort to provide those who might be interested with a few primary documents that shed light on the writer as well as the hunter, but mostly on a compassionate and unique human being. Corbett was no saint and it would do him a disservice to airbrush away the prejudices and paternalism of his time. He loved India, as much for its people as for its forests and wildlife, but he wasn't happy that the British left in 1947. With Maggie he moved to Kenya, where the sun had yet to set on the empire. Though Corbett had spent only a few months in England, he remained steadfastly loyal to his Queen and country.

In his biography of Corbett, D.C. Kala does not shy away from portraying his subject as a product and proponent of British rule, though Corbett was far more sensitive to its nuances and failures than most of his contemporaries. Part of this may have been because he was born and raised in India. He also spoke the language of rural Kumaon, both Hindustani and Kumaoni, as well as a smattering of regional dialects. Much has been made of the fact that he was also fluent in the vocabulary of the forest – the alarm calls of birds and beasts, as well as the telltale sounds of a tiger's approach. He was able to convincingly imitate the roar of a tiger, not just to frighten an audience of schoolboys in Nainital, where he often gave talks about wildlife, but with enough authenticity to call up a man-eater.

MUSSOORIE, AUGUST 2021

Bibliography

Beyts, Ruby. "Recollections of Jim Corbett by Maggie Corbett". Unpublished ms., 1960 (?)

Booth, Martin. *Carpet Sahib.* Delhi: Oxford University Press, 1990.

Doyle, Charles. *The Taming of the Jungle.* Philadelphia: J.B. Lippincott, 1899.

Corbett, Jim. *Jungle Stories.* Naini Tal: London Press, 1935.

———. "Last Will and Testament" (unpublished legal document) 1954.

———. *My Kumaon: Uncollected Writings.* Delhi: Oxford University Press, 2012.

———. *Man-eaters of Kumaon.* London: Oxford University Press, 1944.

Gadhvi, Priyavrat, *et al. Behind Jim Corbett's Stories: An Analytical Journey to "Corbett's Places" and Unanswered Questions, Vol. 1 & 2.* Tblisi: Logos, 2016.

Hawkins, R.E. *Jim Corbett's India.* Delhi: Oxford University Press, 1979.

Kala, D.C. *Jim Corbett of Kumaon.* Delhi: Ravi Dayal and Penguin Books, 2009.

——. "The Hailey National Park". *Hindustan Times Weekly,* 27 June 1954.

Kala, G.R. *Memoirs of the Raj.* Delhi: Mukul Prakashan, 1974.

AKSHAY SHAH is an outdoor educator, a wilderness medicine instructor and a naturalist based in Ranikhet, Uttarakhand. He is currently Director of the Hanifl Centre for Outdoor Education and Environmental Study, Woodstock School, Mussoorie, Uttarakhand.

STEPHEN ALTER is the author of more than twenty books, many of which focus on the natural history of the Himalaya. He lives in Mussoorie, Uttarakhand, and has written a novel about Jim Corbett, *In the Jungles of the Night*.